The *Wisdom*
of MR. CHESTERTON

The *Wisdom*
of Mr. Chesterton

The Very Best
Quips, Quotes, and Cracks
from the Pen of G.K. Chesterton

Edited by DAVE ARMSTRONG

ISBN: 978-1-935302-19-3

Cover Design by Christopher J. Pelicano

For related reading on the author's blog, see the following
web page:
G. K. Chesterton: The "Colossal Genius"
http://socrates58.blogspot.com/2006/04/gk-chesterton-
colossal-genius-links.html

Printed and Bound in the United States of America

Saint Benedict Press, LLC
Charlotte, North Carolina
2009

To G. K. Chesterton: surely one of the most
   insightful men who ever lived.

"A wise man is mightier than a strong man, and a
   man of knowledge than he who has strength."
                                        —*Proverbs 24:5*

$\mathcal{T}$he proverb, however, like many other widely quoted maxims, is really as true as is consistent with meaning nearly the opposite of what it says.

And it has often been more to the advantage of a man to say one good thing in one sentence than to say twenty good things in two thousand sentences.

(All I Survey, ch. 30)

I never read a line of Christian apologetics. I read as little as I can of them now.

(Orthodoxy, ch. 6)

Contents

Introduction

*A*n aphorism is a terse, pithy, astute, proverb-like saying that comments on some general truth; a maxim; an adage. G. K. Chesterton was an absolute master of the form: one of the very best in the English language. His common sense, whimsy and wit, essential optimism, characteristic joviality, and deep Catholic faith further enrich his already wise aphorisms.

Bessie Graham cogently described Chesterton in this regard: "Chesterton is a master of paradox. His style is brilliantly clever and full of aphorisms, which are usually platitudes said backwards, or stood on their heads, as he himself expresses it, to attract attention."[1]

Biographer Maisie Ward delightfully caught the essence of Chesterton's peculiar gift:

> I think nearly all his paradoxes were either the startling expression of an entirely neglected truth, or the startling re-emphasis of the neglected side of a truth. Once, he said: "It is a paradox, but it is God, and not I, who should have the credit of it." . . . [P]aradox must be of the nature of things because of God's infinity and the

---

[1] *Bookman's Manual: A Guide to Literature* (New York: R. R. Bowker Co., 1921, 220)

limitations of the world and of man's mind. To us limited beings God can express His idea only in fragments. We can bring together apparent contradictions in those fragments whereby a greater truth is suggested. If we do this in a sudden or incongruous manner we startle the unprepared and arouse the cry of paradox. But if we will not do it we shall miss a great deal of truth.

Chesterton also saw many proverbs and old sayings as containing a truth which the people who constantly repeated them had forgotten. The world was asleep and must be awakened. The world had gone placidly mad and must be violently restored to sanity. That the methods he used annoyed some is undeniable, but he did force people to think, even if they raged at him as the unaccustomed muscles came into play.[2]

In this semi-comprehensive collection, the following self-imposed requirements determined inclusion:

1. Selections must be single, complete sentences (not just portions of sentences; that is, a clause).
2. The aphorisms (almost by definition) must have a general application, even if specifics are mentioned.
3. Selected aphorisms must stand on their own as more or less complete thoughts or ideas.

I present the citations in the order they appear in Chesterton's works, and chronologically from one work to the next, so that development in Chesterton's thought over time can be observed. Anyone can conveniently access these primary writings via my own Chesterton web page, and track down more details, such as a fuller context or (if provided) a page number, by following the book links there.

[2]*Gilbert Keith Chesterton* (New York: Sheed & Ward, 1943, Chapter XI)

I hope you enjoy reading these quotations as much as I enjoyed compiling them. It's a rich feast for intellect and spirit.

Chesterton Aphorisms

Abortion

If the mother and the baby are both independent individuals, the mother must be as independent of the baby as the baby of the mother; and the mother must be free to say, "I do not like this individual," and throw the baby out of the window.

(ILN, "Being Bored With Ideas," 3-13-26)

Even the most commercial cities of antiquity, like Tyre and Carthage, were not so lively and entertaining when they were making out bills-of-lading or recording the fluctuation of the shekel as compared with the drachma, as when the more poetic side of their nature led them to throw babies into the furnace of Moloch.

(ILN, "The Preservation of the Cities," 8-7-26)

Unless we have a moral principle about such delicate matters as marriage and murder, the whole world will become a welter of exceptions with no rules.

There will be so many hard cases that everything will go soft.

But I do insist that they will be murdered, sooner or later, if we accept in every department the principle of the easiest way out.
(ILN, "The New Immoral Philosophy," 9-21-29)

Suppose something of the type of Compulsory Sterilisation or Compulsory Contraception really stalks through the modern State, leading the march of human progress through abortion to infanticide.

If the English received it, they would accept it as law-abiding citizens; that is, as something between well-trained servants and bewildered children.
(WEL, "Where is the Paradox?")

[see also: Abstinence, Birth Control, Contraception, Eugenics, Euphemisms, Euthanasia, Family, Feminism, Home, Motherhood, Sexuality]

Abstinence

In fact, the whole theory of the Church on virginity might be symbolised in the statement that white is a colour: not merely the absence of a colour.
(O, ch. 6)

Chastity does not mean abstention from sexual wrong; it means something flaming, like Joan of Arc.
(TRE, ch. 2)

Everybody has always known about birth-control, even if it took the wild and unthinkable form of self-control.
(ILN, "The Friends of Frankness, and Euphemism,"
6-30-28)

[see also: Birth Control, Contraception, Marriage, Sexuality]

Adventure

The supreme adventure is being born.
(H, ch. 14)

An adventure is only an inconvenience rightly considered.
(ATC, ch. 4)

Man must have just enough faith in himself to have adventures, and just enough doubt of himself to enjoy them.
(O, ch. 7)

[see also: Children, Fairy-Tales, Imagination, Mythology, Nature, Romanticism, Stories, Wonder]

Agnosticism

When he drops one doctrine after another in a refined scepticism, when he declines to tie himself to a system, when he says that he has outgrown definitions, when he says that he disbelieves in finality, when, in his own imagination, he sits as God, holding no form of creed but contemplating all, then he is by that very process sinking slowly backwards into the vagueness of the vagrant animals and the unconsciousness of the grass.

Trees have no dogmas.
(H, ch. 20)

Many a magnanimous Moslem and chivalrous Crusader must have been nearer to each other, because they were both dogmatists, than any two homeless agnostics in a pew of Mr. Campbell's chapel.
(WWW, I-3)

It would be much truer to say that agnosticism is the origin of all religions.

That is true; the agnostic is at the beginning not the end of human progress.
(AWD, "Something" [1910])

The agnostics have been driven back on agnosticism; and are already recovering from the shock.
(NJ, ch. 8)

It is the business of the agnostic to admit that he knows nothing; and he might the more gracefully admit it touching sciences about which he knows precious little.
(ILN, "Mr Mencken and the New Physics," 6-14-30)

We need not deny that modern doubt, like ancient doubt, does ask deep questions; we only deny that, as compared with our own philosophy, it gives any deeper answers.
(WEL, "The Well and the Shallows")

[see also: Atheism, Authority, Darwinism, Determinism, Hedonism, "Higher Criticism," Liberalism (Theological), Materialism, Modernism, Physics (Modern), Pragmatism, Progress (Idea of), Rebellion, Science, Secularism, Skepticism, Utopias]

Alcohol; Drunkenness

The one genuinely dangerous and immoral way of drinking wine is to drink it as a medicine.

Never drink because you need it, for this is rational drinking, and the way to death and hell.

But drink because you do not need it, for this is irrational drinking, and the ancient health of the world.

(H, ch. 7)

The man who drinks ordinarily makes nothing but an ordinary man of himself.

The man who drinks excessively makes a devil of himself.

(CD, ch. 9)

The real case against drunkenness is not that it calls up the beast, but that it calls up the Devil.

(ILN, "Alcohol, Drunkenness, and Drinking," 4-20-07)

America

There is one thing, at any rate, that must strike all Englishmen who have the good fortune to have

American friends; that is, that while there is no materialism so crude or so material as American materialism, there is also no idealism so crude or so ideal as American idealism.

America will always affect an Englishman as being soft in the wrong place and hard in the wrong place; coarse exactly where all civilised men are delicate, delicate exactly where all grown-up men are coarse.

(CD, ch. 6)

Almost every trait which is specially and solely characteristic of America is a savage trait.

America was the last of the great Christian nations to keep slaves.

America is almost the only one of the great Christian nations in which one can still find primitive private war, shootings and stabbings not under the rules of military service, and not even under the dignity and etiquette of the duel; mere private killing as it might have been among the cave-men.

America is the one place in the modern world which has returned to the hearty old human custom of burning a man alive in public.

America is the one place in the modern world in which there is a mere race-war, a war uncomplicated by any question of religion, undignified by any principle of patriotism, a mere brutal war of breed against breed, of black against white.

But men burn a Negro as they burn an old hat; because they dislike the physical notion of his having anything to do with them.

   (ILN, "America and Barbarism," 2-16-07)

I am, I believe, one of the few Englishmen who really love and respect Americans; I love that old-world simplicity which makes their minds like ancient crystals.

   (ILN, "Objections to Spiritualism," 10-30-09)

And the American has become so idealistic that he even idealises money.

   (TRE, ch. 31)

[see also: Ireland, Scotland]

Anarchy

Complete anarchy would not merely make it impossible to have any discipline or fidelity; it would also make it impossible to have any fun.

   (O, ch. 7)

Anarchy is that condition of mind or methods in which you cannot stop yourself.

It is the loss of that self-control which can return to the normal.

It is not anarchy to have a picnic; but it is anarchy to lose all memory of mealtimes.

It is this inability to return within rational limits after a legitimate extravagance that is the really dangerous disorder.

   (EUG, I-3)

[see also: Aristocracy, Caesaropapism, Conservatism, Democracy, Government, Law, Liberalism (Political), Monarchy, Nationalism, Nazism, Patriotism, Politicians, Revolution, Socialism, Spain (Civil War), Tolerance, Voting]

Angels

Angels can fly because they can take themselves lightly.

(O, ch. 7)

Men, they say, are now imitating angels; in their flying-machines, that is: not in any other respect that I have heard of.

(AD, ch. 28)

[see also: Cross, Death, Evil, Ghosts, Incarnation, Jesus, Mary, Mass, Miracles, Original Sin, Resurrection, Sacramentalism, Saints, Satan & Demons, Sin, Transubstantiation, Trinitarianism]

Animal Rights; Humane Treatment of Animals

I reject all talk about animals having the same rights as human beings, all talk about our having no moral right to kill or control them, all talk of their being perhaps better than we, all talk of the only division between us and them being the fact that they are "dumb"; which they are not.

(ILN, "Undergraduate Ragging," 12-28-07)

We may eventually be bound not to disturb a man's mind even by argument; not to disturb the sleep of birds even by coughing.

The ultimate apotheosis would appear to be that of a man sitting quite still, nor daring to stir for fear of disturbing a fly, nor to eat for fear of incommoding a microbe.

(O, ch. 7)

The truth is, obviously, that the man ought to be kind to the dog, not because he is entirely unified and absorbed and melted into the dog, but precisely because he has himself a dignity and a duty that cannot be expected of the dog, far less of the wolf.

(ILN, "The So-Called Unity of Living Things," 6-18-27)

If there is no authority in things which Christendom has called moral, because their origins were mystical, then they are clearly free to ignore all difference between animals and men; and treat men as we treat animals.

(WEL, "Babies and Distributism")

[see also: Abortion, Environmentalism, Euthanasia, Man, Morality, Vegetarianism]

Anthropology

That same suppression of sympathies, that same waving away of intuitions or guess-work which make a man preternaturally clever in dealing with the stomach of a spider, will make him preternaturally stupid in dealing with the heart of man.

He is making himself inhuman in order to understand humanity.

For the secrets about which anthropologists concern themselves can be best learnt, not from books or voyages, but from the ordinary commerce of man with man.

If a man desires to find out the origins of religions, let him not go to the Sandwich Islands; let him go to church.

The man of science, not realizing that ceremonial is essentially a thing which is done without a reason, has to find a reason for every sort of ceremonial, and, as might be supposed, the reason is generally a very absurd one—absurd because it originates not in the simple mind of the barbarian, but in the sophisticated mind of the professor.

Possibly the most pathetic of all the delusions of the modern students of primitive belief is the notion they have about the thing they call anthropomorphism.

They believe that primitive men attributed phenomena to a god in human form in order to explain them, because his mind in its sullen limitation could not reach any further than his own clownish existence.

(H, ch. 11)

Sometimes the professor with his bone becomes almost as dangerous as a dog with his bone.

A man of the future finding the ruins of our factory machinery might as fairly say that we were acquainted with iron and with no other substance; and announce the discovery that the proprietor and manager of the factory undoubtedly walked about naked—or possibly wore iron hats and trousers.

(EM, I-2)

[see also: Ceremony, Compartmentalization, Customs, Environment, Man, Man (Smallness of), Nationality, Sociology]

Anti-Catholicism

But a mob cries out "No Popery"; it does not cry out "Not so much Popery," still less "Only a moderate admixture of Popery."

(NJ, ch. 7)

All that early and sensational picture of the sins of Rome always seemed to me silly even when I was a boy or an unbeliever; and I cannot describe how I passed out of it because I was never in it.

It must either mean that they suspect that our religion has something about it so wrong that the hint of it is bad for anybody; or else that it has something so right that the presence of it would convert anybody.

A shade more plausible than the notion that Popish priests merely seek after evil was the notion that they are exceptionally ready to seek good by means of evil.

In vulgar language, it is the notion that if they are not sensual they are always sly.

I noticed that those who were most ready to blame priests for relying on rigid formulas seldom took the trouble to find out what the formulas were.

It puzzled me very much, even at that early stage, to imagine why people bringing controversial charges against a powerful and prominent institution should thus neglect to test their own case, and should draw in this random way on their own imagination.

I never dreamed that the Roman religion was true; but I knew that its accusers, for some reason or other, were curiously inaccurate.

(CCC, ch. 2)

These stale stories seem to count for a great deal with people who are resolved to keep far away from the Church.

(CCC, ch. 3)

Some part of the difficulty is doubtless due to the odd way in which so many people are at once preoccupied with it and prejudiced against it.

It is queer to observe so much ignorance with so little indifference.

They love talking about it and they hate hearing about it.

I fancy that there is more than meets the eye in this curious controversial attitude; the desire to ask rhetorical questions and not to ask real questions; the wish to heckle and not to hear.

(TT, ch. 9)

There is always some such medley of misused words, in which mitres, misereres, nones, albs, croziers, virgins and viaticums tumble over each other without the wildest hope that anybody could possibly know what any of them mean.

(WEL, "Levity – or Levitation")

A writer on a High Church paper, being full of the lyric muse, recently described me as a "prolix Papist professor of paradox"; a line which it is my firm intention to extend into a poem of no less than nine verses depending upon the letter p; by which alliterative industry the unaccountable absence of any allusion to polygamous Popes, poisoning Pontiffs, piratical prelates and pestilent peasantries, will be supplied and made good at my own expense.

(WEL, "Where is the Paradox?")

[see also: Bigotry, Calvinism, dogmatism, Private Judgment, Protestantism, Prejudice, Puritanism, Reformation (English), Reformation (Protestant), Religion (Comparative), Tolerance]

Apologetics

What we want just now more than anything else is people who really can exhibit old truths in new form.

(ILN, "The New Theology and Modern Thought," 3-23-07)

It is very hard for a man to defend anything of which he is entirely convinced.

(O, ch. 6)

And the paradox is this; that we never find our own religion so right as when we find we are wrong about it.

I mean that we are finally convinced not by the sort of evidence we are looking for, but by the sort of evidence we are not looking for.

We are convinced when we come on a ratification that is almost as abrupt as a refutation.

(NJ, ch. 9)

Our enemies no longer really know how to attack the faith; but that is no reason why we should not know how to defend it.

I do not object to laymen proselytising; for I never could see, even when I was practically a pagan, why a man should not urge his own opinions if he liked and that opinion as much as any other.

(CCC, ch. 3)

I believe there is a very urgent need for a verbal paraphrase of many of the fundamental doctrines; simply because people have ceased to understand them as they are traditionally stated.

(TT, ch. 26)

It is no good to tell an atheist that he is an atheist; or to charge a denier of immortality with the infamy of denying it; or to imagine that one can force an opponent to admit he is wrong, by proving that he is wrong on somebody else's principles, but not on his own.

After the great example of St. Thomas, the principle stands, or ought always to have stood established; that we must either not argue with a man at all, or we must argue on his grounds and not ours.

(STA, ch. 3)

As an apologist I am the reverse of apologetic.

(A, ch. 4)

[see also: Argument, Faith (and Reason), Ideas, Idealism, Paradox (in Christianity), Philosophy, Reason & Logic, Science (and Religion), Theism, Truth]

Architecture

Architecture is a very good test of the true strength of a society, for the most valuable things in a human state are the irrevocable things—marriage, for instance.

(TRE, ch. 9)

And so also there are buildings that are shapeless in their strength, seeming to lift themselves slowly like monsters from the primal mire, and there are spires that seem to fly up suddenly like a startled bird.

(TRE, ch. 18)

All architecture is great architecture after sunset; perhaps architecture is really a nocturnal art, like the art of fireworks.

(TRE, ch. 20)

Vandalism is of two kinds, the negative and the positive; as in the Vandals of the ancient world, who destroyed buildings, and the Vandals of the modern world, who erect them.

(CM, "Vandalism")

[see also: Art and Artists, Cathedrals, Cities, Middle Ages, Poetry, Writers]

Argument; Dialogue; Debate; Disputation

This desire to meet and argue for hours is a male peculiarity.

(ILN, "Women, Camaraderie, and Politics," 5-26-06)

It is an almost invariable rule that the man with whom I don't agree thinks I am making a fool of myself, and the man with whom I do agree thinks I am making a fool of him.

(ILN, "Spiritualism and Frivolity," 6-9-06)

Even prejudice is saner than sophistry.
                    (ILN, "Arguing With Erudition," 10-31-08)

This is the essential idea, that all good argument consists in beginning with the indisputable thing and then disputing everything else in the light of it.
                    (ILN, "Taking Reason by the Right End," 11-7-08)

Any one setting out to dispute anything ought always to begin by saying what he does not dispute.
                                        (O, ch. 1)

Personally, I fear that this same decadence which treats men as dogs in argument will treat them like dogs in practice.
                    (ILN, "Socialistic Morality," 3-26-10)

Genuine controversy, fair cut and thrust before a common audience, has become in our special epoch very rare.

For the sincere controversialist is above all things a good listener.

The really burning enthusiast never interrupts; he listens to the enemy's arguments as eagerly as a spy would listen to the enemy's arrangements.

But if you attempt an actual argument with a modern paper of opposite politics, you will find that no medium is admitted between violence and evasion.
                                        (WWW, I-3)

This doctrine of equality is essential to conversation; so much may be admitted by anyone who knows what conversation is.

Once arguing at a table in a tavern the most famous man on earth would wish to be obscure, so that his brilliant remarks might blaze like the stars on the background of his obscurity.

To anything worth calling a man nothing can be conceived more cold or cheerless than to be king of your company.

(WWW, II-3)

I fear it is more often the motive that creates the argument than the argument that creates the motive.
(ILN, "The Refusal to Understand," 4-24-26)

Only, as is commonly the case today, hardly anybody makes any attempt at defining the thing he is always denouncing, finding it much easier to denounce than to define.
(ILN, "On Sentimentalism," 8-20-27)

But as a fact, men for the most part vastly prefer to dispute about taste, because they do not want their disputes settled.
(ILN, "Disputes About Artistic Tastes," 12-17-27)

It is astonishing to note how often, when we address a man with anything resembling an idea, he answers with some recognised metaphor, supposed to be appropriate to the case.
(ILN, "Myths and Metaphors," 1-26-29)

Nothing is so bright and cheering as a hostile statement that is really to the point; an opponent who does
really see the point, even if he points at it in derision.
        (ILN, "England and Dogmatic Christianity," 2-9-29)

People generally quarrel because they cannot argue.

People do not seem to understand even the first principle of all argument: that people must agree in order to
disagree.

Each party expresses his or her feelings, as if nothing
were needed but the artistic experience of self-expression.

Debate is now a thing of personalities, sometimes of
very agreeable personalities; but if it were less personal
and more impersonal it would be more practical and to
the point.
        (ILN, "The New Generations and Morality," 3-9-29)

But they were quite incapable of seeing where their
own line of argument was leading them; and I have found
that this particular sort of blindness is very much more
prevalent than I had myself supposed; perhaps, much
more prevalent than the alternative of sight.
        (ILN, "On Arguing in a Straight Line," 6-21-30)

I do not find men now so eager to prove things, but,
at most, to assure me that they have been proved.

It is an age of Suggestion; that is, of appeal to the
irrational part of man.
        (ILN, "The Laziness of the Modern Intellect," 10-11-30)

What I object to is one of the debaters coolly announcing at the start that everybody in the world thinks as he does, or that anybody in the world who thinks differently does not think at all.

Only certain opinions were called enlightened opinions; only certain policies were called enlightened policies; as if it were not a question of convictions being held, but merely of concrete facts being seen; and that, if they were once seen; there were no two opinions about them.

(ILN, "On Assuming Too Much in Debate," 8-22-31)

Indeed, I think there are fewer people now alive who understand argument than there were twenty or thirty years ago; and St. Thomas might have preferred the society of the atheists of the early nineteenth century to that of the blank sceptics of the early twentieth.

As a matter of fact, it is generally the man who is not ready to argue, who is ready to sneer.

(STA, ch. 5)

Perhaps the principal objection to a quarrel is that it interrupts an argument.

(A, ch. 9)

[see also: Apologetics, Faith (and Reason), Ideas, Idealism, Paradox (in Christianity), Philosophy, Reason & Logic, Science (and Religion), Theism, Truth]

Aristocracy

The evil of aristocracy is not that it necessarily leads to the infliction of bad things or the suffering of sad ones; the evil of aristocracy is that it places everything in the hands of a class of people who can always inflict what they can never suffer.

The case against them simply is that when they legislate for all men, they always omit themselves.

(H, ch. 19)

In England we have an aristocracy instead of a religion.

In the same way in England we have an aristocracy instead of a Government.

(ATC, ch. 16)

The great and very obvious merit of the English aristocracy is that nobody could possibly take it seriously.

(O, ch. 7)

The god of the aristocrats is not tradition, but fashion, which is the opposite of tradition.

(WWW, I-10)

Living in a country where aristocracy does not exist, he had a high opinion of it.

(AD, ch. 17)

[see also: Anarchy, Caesaropapism, Conservatism, Democracy, Government, Law, Liberalism (Political), Monarchy, Nationalism, Nazism, Patriotism, Politicians, Revolution, Socialism, Spain (Civil War), Tolerance, Voting]

Art and Artists

Nothing sublimely artistic has ever arisen out of mere art, any more than anything essentially reasonable has ever arisen out of the pure reason.

There must always be a rich moral soil for any great aesthetic growth.

(DEF, ch. 5)

But the truth of the matter is, that an artist teaches far more by his mere background and properties, his landscape, his costume, his idiom and technique—all the part of his work, in short, of which he is probably entirely unconscious, than by the elaborate and pompous moral dicta which he fondly imagines to be his opinions.

(TWE, ch. 10)

Any man with a vital knowledge of the human psychology ought to have the most profound suspicion of anybody who claims to be an artist, and talks a great deal about art.

Art is a right and human thing, like walking or saying one's prayers; but the moment it begins to be talked about very solemnly, a man may be fairly certain that the thing has come into a congestion and a kind of difficulty.

(H, ch. 17)

A man cannot be wise enough to be a great artist without being wise enough to wish to be a philosopher.

A man cannot have the energy to produce good art without having the energy to wish to pass beyond it.

A small artist is content with art; a great artist is content with nothing except everything.

(H, ch. 20)

In spite of the tiresome half-truth that art is unmoral, the arts require a certain considerable number of moral qualities, and more especially all the arts require courage.

(VT, ch. 20)

Exaggeration is the definition of art.

(CD, ch. 1)

Tolstoy is never more admirable than when declaring that art ought not to be the mysterious amusement of a clique, but the obvious self-expression of men: art is a language, and not a secret language.

(ILN, "A Uniform Creed For Humanity," 10-3-08)

The most beautiful part of every picture is the frame.

(TRE, ch. 23)

The good artist is he who can be understood; it is the bad artist who is always "misunderstood."

(ILN, "The Bonds of Love," 7-2-10)

The romance of ritual and colored emblem has been taken over by that narrowest of all trades, modern art (the sort called art for art's sake), and men are in modern practice informed that they may use all symbols so long as they mean nothing by them.

(WWW, III-2)

Modern art has to be what is called "intense."

(AD, ch. 38)

They circulate a piece of paper on which Mr. Picasso has had the misfortune to upset the ink and tried to dry it with his boots, and they seek to terrify democracy by the good old anti-democratic muddlements: that "the public" does not understand these things; that "the likes of us" cannot dare to question the dark decisions of our lords.

If the art critics can say nothing about the artists except that they are good it is because the artists are bad.

(MM, ch. 21)

That an artist could produce better art because he was lawless is very far from being obvious and very far from being proved.

(ILN, "The Defense of the Unconventional," 10-17-25)

Art is the signature of man.

Every true artist does feel, consciously or unconsciously, that he is touching transcendental truths; that his images are shadows of things seen through the veil.

Nobody understands it who has not had what can only be called the ache of the artist to find some sense

and some story in the beautiful things he sees; his hunger for secrets and his anger at any tower or tree escap-
ing with its tale untold.

(EM, I-5)

The artist does ultimately exhibit himself as being
intelligent by being intelligible.

But if all he can say is that he has a secret of
sealed-up power and passion, that his imagination is visited by visions of which the world knows nothing, that he
is conscious of a point of view which is wholly his own and
is not expressed in anything common or comprehensible
– then he is simply saying that he is *not* an artist, and
there is an end to it.

It is when the work has passed from mind to mind
that it becomes a work of art.

(ILN, "Progress in the Arts," 11-27-26)

The dignity of the artist lies in his duty of keeping
awake the sense of wonder in the world.

(ILN, "The Falling Value of Words," 5-21-27)

It would be rather truer to say that Art can be
immoral, but cannot be unmoral.

(ILN, "On Unmoral Comedy," 12-10-27)

The cinema is a machine for unrolling certain regular
patterns called pictures; expressing the most vulgar millionaires' notion of the taste of the most vulgar millions.

(WEL, "Babies and Distributism")

[see also: Architecture, Cathedrals, Fiction, Imagination, Poetry, Renaissance, Romanticism, Stories,
Writers]

Artificiality

Nothing in the world has ever been artificial.

Many customs, many dresses, many works of art are
branded with artificiality because they exhibit vanity and
self-consciousness: as if vanity were not a deep and elemental thing, like love and hate and the fear of death.

(TWE, ch. 3)

Asceticism

But asceticism is not in the least confined to religious asceticism: there is scientific asceticism which
asserts that truth is alone satisfying: there is aesthetic
asceticism which asserts that art is alone satisfying:
there is amatory asceticism which asserts that love is
alone satisfying.

We insist that the ascetics were pessimists because
they gave up threescore years and ten for an eternity of
happiness.

We forget that the bare proposition of an eternity of
happiness is by its very nature ten thousand times more
optimistic than ten thousand pagan saturnalias.

(TWE, ch. 5)

I say that the main Christian impulse cannot be described as asceticism, even in the ascetics.

(H, ch. 12)

They were ascetic because asceticism was the only possible purge of the sins of the world; but in the very thunder of their anathemas they affirmed for ever that their asceticism was not to be anti-human or anti-natural; that they did wish to purge the world and not destroy it.

(EM, II-4)

If ascetics have given up love or liberty, it is not because these things are not valuable, but because they are.

(ILN, "England and Dogmatic Christianity," 2-9-29)

Any extreme of Catholic asceticism is a wise, or unwise, precaution against the evil of the Fall; it is *never* a doubt about the good of the Creation.

(STA, ch. 4)

[see also: Confession, Faith, Gnosticism, Incense, Martyrdom, Mysticism, Relics, Robes, Sabbath, Temptation]

Atheism

But the materialist's world is quite simple and solid, just as the madman is quite sure he is sane.

(O, ch. 2)

An atheist and a theist only differ by a single letter; yet theologians are so subtle as to distinguish definitely between the two.

(NJ, ch. 6)

The intellect exercises itself in discovering principles of design or pattern or proportion of some sort, and can find nothing to work on in the only really logical atheist cosmos – the fortuitous concourse of atoms of Lucretius.

(ILN, "A Defense of Human Dignity," 2-22-30)

[see also: Agnosticism, Authority, Darwinism, Determinism, Hedonism, "Higher Criticism," Liberalism (Theological), Materialism, Modernism, Physics (Modern), Pragmatism, Progress (Idea of), Rebellion, Science, Secularism, Skepticism, Utopias]

Authority

The general rule is that nothing must be accepted on any ancient or admitted authority, but everything must be accepted on any new or nameless authority, or accepted even more eagerly on no authority at all.

(ILN, "Quackery About the Family," 7-12-30)

I was never able to accept this highly modern and credulous conception; because I am unable to imagine any human being accepting any authority that he has not originally reached by reason.

(AS, ch. 5)

Authority, Religious

But the modern critics of religious authority are like men who should attack the police without ever having heard of burglars.

(O, ch. 3)

[see also: Catholicism & Catholics, Catholicity, Christianity, Church (Catholic), Conversion (Catholic), Development (Doctrinal), Dogma (Catholic), History (Church), Orthodoxy, Paganism (and Christianity), Papacy & Popes, Protestantism, Reformation (Catholic), Religion (Organized), Theologians, Tradition]

Automobiles

Doubtless the duke now feels it as necessary to have a motor as to have a roof, and in a little while he may feel it equally necessary to have a flying ship.

To me personally, at least, it would never seem needful to own a motor, any more than to own an avalanche.

But about motoring there is something magical, like going to the moon; and I say the thing should be kept exceptional and felt as something breathless and bizarre.

And what is true of the old freaks of wealth, flavour and fierce colour and smell, I would say also of the new freak of wealth, which is speed.

(AD, ch. 26)

Doubtless the unsympathetic might state my doctrine that one should not own a motor like a horse, but rather use it like a flying dragon in the simpler form that I will always go motoring in somebody else's car.

(AD, ch. 27)

It is one of the rare merits of modern mechanical travel that it enables us to compare widely different cities in rapid succession.

(NJ, ch. 1)

Many, but ill-acquainted with my habits, seem to suppose that I recoil in horror from a motor-car and insist on being wheeled about, like Mr. Pickwick, in a wheelbarrow.

(AS, ch. 4)

[see also: Capitalism, Cities, Communications, Hustle & Bustle, Inventions, Traffic]

Bible, The

Those are wrong who maintain that the Old Testament is a mere loose library; that it has no consistency or aim.

Whether the result was achieved by some supernal spiritual truth, or by a steady national tradition, or merely by an ingenious selection in aftertimes, the books of the Old Testament have a quite perceptible unity.

God is not the only chief character of the Old Testament; God is properly the only character in the Old Testament.

(JOB)

We know that if the authors of the Revised Version knew more about Hebrew, the authors of the Authorised Version knew much more about English.

(ILN, "Arguing With Erudition," 10-31-08)

But it is unfair to turn round and blame the Bible because of all these legends and jokes and journalistic allusions, which are read into the Bible by people who have not read the Bible.

(ILN, "The Bible and the Sceptics," 4-20-29)

[see also: "Higher Criticism," Prophets, Revelation (Book of), *Sola Scriptura*]

Bigotry and Racism

And of all the forms in which science, or pseudo-science, has come to the rescue of the rich and stupid, there is none so singular as the singular invention of the theory of races.

When a wealthy nation like the English discovers the perfectly patent fact that it is making a ludicrous mess of the government of a poorer nation like the Irish, it pauses for a moment in consternation, and then begins to talk about Celts and Teutons.

(H, ch. 13)

In real life the people who are most bigoted are the people who have no convictions at all.

Bigotry may be roughly defined as the anger of men who have no opinions.

Bigotry may be called the appalling frenzy of the indifferent.

Bigotry in the main has always been the pervading omnipotence of those who do not care crushing out those who care in darkness and blood.

(H, ch. 20)

The old bigot said, "I will argue with you because I know you are wrong; I will even kill you because I know you disagree with me."

The new bigot says, "I will not argue with you because I know you agree with me."
(ILN, "Bigotry in the Modern World," 4-28-06)

Modern hostility is a base thing, and arises, not out of a generous difference, but out of a sort of bitter and sneering similarity.
(ILN, "On the World Getting Smaller," 5-9-08)

One can meet an assertion with argument; but healthy bigotry is the only way in which one can meet a tendency.
(WWW, I-3)

The bigot is not he who knows he is right; every sane man knows he is right.

The bigot is he whose emotions and imagination are too cold and weak to feel how it is that other men go wrong.
(AD, ch. 19)

It is the vice of any patriotism or religion depending on race that the individual is himself the thing to be worshipped; the individual is his own ideal, and even his own idol.

(NJ, ch. 2)

Bigotry consists in a man being convinced that another man must be wrong in everything, because he is wrong in a particular belief; that he must be wrong, even in thinking that he honestly believes he is right.

(CM, "The New Bigotry")

[see also: Broadmindedness, Conspiratorialism, Dogmatism, Openmindedness, Prejudice, Tolerance]

Birth Control

Everybody has always exercised birth-control, even when they were so paradoxical as to permit the process to end in a birth.

(ILN, "The Friends of Frankness, and Euphemism," 6-30-28)

They insist on talking about Birth Control when they mean less birth and no control.

(TT, ch. 6)

It is in fact, of course, a scheme for preventing birth in order to escape control.

(WEL, "The Surrender Upon Sex")

The proceeding these quack doctors recommend does not control any birth.

It only makes sure that there shall never be any birth to control.

(WEL, "Babies and Distributism")

[see also: Abortion, Abstinence, Contraception, Eugenics, Euphemisms, Euthanasia, Family, Feminism, Home, Motherhood, Sexuality]

Boredom

There is no such thing on earth as an uninteresting subject; the only thing that can exist is an uninterested person.

(H, ch. 3)

Monotony has nothing to do with a place; monotony, either in its sensation or its infliction, is simply the quality of a person.

(AD, ch. 39)

Byron, I think, divided men into the bores and the bored, presumably priding himself on being among the latter, and through that very pride occasionally figuring among the former.

(ILN, "Introverts and Extroverts," 7-19-30)

Bravery

Only the weak can be brave; and yet again, in practice, only those who can be brave can be trusted, in time of doubt, to be strong.

(H, ch. 5)

Broadmindedness

Or have we only learnt to spread our thoughts thinner?

(TWE, ch. 4)

Turnips are singularly broad-minded.

(H, ch. 20)

There is no person so narrow as the person who is
sure that he is broad; indeed, being quite *sure* that one is
broad is itself a form of narrowness.

(ILN, "Bigotry of the Rationalists," 4-30-10)

For that is what is meant to-day by being broadmin-
ded: living on prejudices and never looking at them.

(ILN, "Drawing the Line Somewhere," 5-5-28)

[see also: Bigotry & Racism, Conspiratorialism,
Dogmatism, Openmindedness, Prejudice, Tolerance]

Caesaropapism; State Church

In Russia the one real charge brought by religious people (especially Roman Catholics) against the Orthodox Church is not its orthodoxy or heterodoxy, but its abject dependence on the State.

(EUG, I-7)

Of course, the one thing that has really confused the story of Church and State is the thing called the State Church.

But that is a mere illogical interlude; in which God holds his authority from Caesar; instead of Caesar holding it from God.

(WEL, "The Return of Caesar")

[see also: Anarchy, Aristocracy, Conservatism, Democracy, Government, Law, Liberalism (Political), Monarchy, Nationalism, Nazism, Patriotism, Politicians, Revolution, Socialism, Spain (Civil War), Tolerance, Voting]

Calvinism

The doctrine of Calvinism I take briefly to be this: that the Almighty acts towards mankind as a man acts towards a garden: growing what he chooses, plucking it when he chooses, rooting up what he chooses in the pure irresponsibility of art.

(ILN, "The New Theology and Modern Thought," 3-23-07)

They had assumed the Divine foreknowledge as so fixed, that it must, if necessary, fulfil itself by destroying the Divine mercy.

(TT, ch. 3)

It is the difference between believing that God knows, as a fact, that I choose to go to the devil; and believing that God has given me to the devil, without my having any choice at all.

(TT, ch. 7)

If he believes in a God at all, or even if he does not, he would quite certainly prefer a God who has made all men for joy, and desires to save them all, to a God who deliberately made some for involuntary sin and immortal misery.

(TT, ch. 8)

The old Manicheans taught that Satan originated the whole work of creation commonly attributed to God.

The new Calvinists taught that God originates the whole work of damnation commonly attributed to Satan.

But both had the idea that the creator of the earth was primarily the creator of the evil, whether we call him a devil or a god.

(STA, ch. 4)

[see also: Anti-Catholicism, Private Judgment, Protestantism, Puritanism, Reformation (English), Reformation (Protestant)]

Capitalism; Commercialism; Economics

Therefore there has arisen in modern life a literary fashion devoting itself to the romance of business, to great demigods of greed and to fairyland of finance.

(WWW, II-4)

This sane distinction of sentiment is not instinctive at present, because our standard of life is that of the governing class, which is eternally turning luxuries into necessities as fast as pork is turned into sausages; and which cannot remember the beginning of its needs and cannot get to the end of its novelties.

(AD, ch. 26)

But it certainly is the fact that his economic position as a modern wage-earner is less secure even than his position when he was a feudal serf, and far less dignified than when he had the luck to be a free guildsman.

If I say that there is at least a doubt, touching the mass of men, whether their lot has been improved at all by the vast rational revolution of the last four hundred years, I am deliberately adopting a tone of restraint and even of understatement.

What they have done is to destroy charity for the sake of competition, and then to turn their own competition into monopoly.

What they have done is to turn both peasants and guildsmen into the employed, and then turn these into the unemployed.

They trampled on a hundred humanities of piety and pity in order to rush after Free Trade; and their Free Trade has been so free that it has brought them within a stride of the Servile State.

(ROC, Epilogue)

Peasants have lived side by side in practical equality for countless centuries, without one of them buying up the rest or the rest becoming servants of the one.

(ILN, "Capitalism and Real Ownership," 3-31-23)

Now, nine-tenths of the modern social reform as worked out in Utopias and ideal republics consists, quite coldly and literally, in treating a man like a dog.

(ILN, "The Leisure State and the Liberty State," 7-14-23)

Personally I think the Socialist and the Capitalist are very much alike, especially in the great unifying quality of being both wrong.

(ILN, "Eliminating the Class Without Property," 11-8-24)

The thing called Capitalism which all Socialists are now denouncing is practically the very thing that all radicals were once demanding.

(ILN, "Modern Doubts and Questioning," 2-13-26)

To take another aspect of the same thing, it is infinitely more likely at this moment that wars will be waged for the possession of oil-fields than it ever was that they would be waged for the possession of hop-fields.

(ILN, "Mr. Ford and Prohibition," 5-22-26)

All centralised systems mean the rule of a few; and industrial machinery is the most centralised of all systems.

(ILN, "Mencken on Democracy," 11-13-26)

When I say "Capitalism," I commonly mean something that may be stated thus: "That economic condition in which there is a class of capitalists, roughly recognizable and relatively small, in whose possession so much of the capital is concentrated as to necessitate a very large majority of the citizens serving those capitalists for a wage."

Now the capitalist system, good or bad, right or wrong, rests upon two ideas: that the rich will always be rich enough to hire the poor; and the poor will always be poor enough to want to be hired.

We have already accepted anything that anybody of intelligence ever disliked in Socialism.

(OS, ch. 1)

It is simply a question of whether we have the moral courage to punish what is certainly immoral.

There is no more doubt about these operations of high finance than there is about piracy on the high seas.

Meanwhile I sit amid droves of overdriven clerks and underpaid workmen in a tube or a tram; I read of the great conception of Men Like Gods and I wonder when men will be like men.

(OS, ch. 6)

The pirate who grew rich on the high seas at least could not be a coward; the pirate who grows rich on the high prices may be that, as well as everything else that is unworthy.

(ILN, "The Real Philosophy of the Abstainer," 1-7-28)

There is less difference than many suppose between the ideal, Socialist system, in which the big businesses are run by the State, and the present Capitalist system, in which the State is run by the big businesses.

(ILN, "The Innocent Conservatism of Youth," 10-27-28)

Men in mediaeval times tolerated more ruthless punishments; men in modern times tolerate more reckless and irresponsible financial speculation and control.

(ILN, "On Fundamental Morality," 12-1-28)

Our fathers hanged men for petty thefts, whereas we only exalt and ennoble men or put them in the House of Lords for really large and impressive thefts.

(AIS, ch. 22)

Whether anything more solid can be built again upon a social philosophy of values, there is now no space to discuss at length here; but I am certain that nothing solid can be built on any other philosophy; certainly not upon the utterly un-philosophical philosophy of blind buying and selling; of bullying people into purchasing what they do not want; of making it badly so that they may break it and imagine they want it again; of keeping rubbish in rapid circulation like a dust-storm in a desert; and pretending that you are teaching men to hope, because you do not leave them one intelligent instant in which to despair.

(WEL, "Reflections on a Rotten Apple")

The two sinister things can be seen side by side in the system of Bolshevist Russia; for Communism is the only complete and logical working model of Capitalism.

(WEL, "Sex and Property")

I will only say that his paean in praise of nineteenth-century capitalism would have been very welcome to the rich in the nineteenth century; and greatly encouraged those who laid on the millions a yoke little better than slavery.

(WEL, "Why Protestants Prohibit")

[see also: Distributism, Guilds, Philanthropy, Poor, Publicity, Simplicity, Socialism, Thrift, Wealth]

Casuistry ("Jesuitical")

The theory attributed to the Jesuits was very often almost identical with the practice adopted by nearly everybody I knew.

Everybody in society practised verbal economies, equivocations and often direct fictions, without any sense of essential falsehood.

Every gentleman was expected to say he would be delighted to dine with a bore; every lady said that somebody else's baby was beautiful if she thought it as ugly as sin: for they did not think it a sin to avoid saying ugly things.

This might be right or wrong; but it was absurd to pillory half a dozen Popish priests for a crime committed daily by half a million Protestant laymen.

The only difference was that the Jesuits had been worried enough about the matter to try to make rules and limitations saving as much verbal veracity as possible; whereas the happy Protestants were not worried about it at all, but told lies from morning to night as merrily and innocently as the birds sing in the trees. The fact is, of course, that the modern world is full of an utterly lawless casuistry because the Jesuits were prevented from making a lawful casuistry.

But every man is a casuist or a lunatic.

(CCC, ch. 2)

[see also: Anti-Catholicism, Morality]

Cathedrals

Greek heroes do not grin: but gargoyles do—because they are Christian.

(O, ch. 7)

But a mass of mediaeval carving seems actually a sort of bustle or hubbub in stone.

Sometimes one cannot help feeling that the groups actually move and mix, and the whole front of a great cathedral has the hum of a huge hive.

(TRE, ch. 30)

The real explanation, I fancy, is this: that these cathedrals and columns of triumph were meant, not for people more cultured and self-conscious than modern tourists, but for people much rougher and more casual.

Those leaps of live stone like frozen fountains, were so placed and poised as to catch the eye of ordinary inconsiderate men going about their daily business; and when they are so seen they are never forgotten.

Buy a bicycle in Maidstone to visit an aunt in Dover, and you will see Canterbury Cathedral as it was built to be seen.

You will appreciate Hereford Cathedral if you have come for cider, not if you have come for architecture.

(AD, ch. 12)

[see also: Architecture, Art and Artists, Cities, Middle Ages, Poetry, Writers]

Catholicism and Catholics

No Catholic thinks he is a good Catholic; or he would by that thought become a bad Catholic.

(WEL, "The Don and the Cavalier")

[see also: Authority (Religious), Catholicity, Christianity, Church (Catholic), Conversion (Catholic), Development (Doctrinal), Dogma (Catholic), History (Church), Orthodoxy, Paganism (and Christianity), Papacy & Popes, Protestantism, Reformation (Catholic), Religion (Organized), Theologians, Tradition]

Catholicity

Now a Catholic, especially a born Catholic, can never understand that attitude, because from the first his whole religion is rooted in the unity of the race of Adam, the one and only Chosen Race.

But just as the relic follows upon the religion, so the local loyalty follows on the universal brotherhood of all men.

We start with mankind and go beyond it to all the varied loves and traditions of mankind.

But it is absurd to treat the Church as a novel conspiracy attacking the State, when the State was only recently a novel experiment arising within the Church.

(CCC, ch. 2)

[see also: Authority (Religious), Catholicism & Catholics, Christianity, Church (Catholic), Conversion (Catholic), Development (Doctrinal), Dogma (Catholic), History (Church), Orthodoxy, Paganism (and Christianity), Papacy & Popes, Protestantism, Reformation (Catholic), Religion (Organized), Theologians, Tradition]

Ceremony and Ritual

All men, then, are ritualists, but are either conscious or unconscious ritualists.

(H, ch. 18)

But, above all, ceremony is a pleasure and a sort of framework for all the arts.

Ceremony is acted poetry.
(ILN, "Education and Half-Education," 6-2-28)

[see also: Anthropology, Compartmentalization, Customs, Environment, Incense, Man, Man (Smallness of), Mass, Nationality, Sociology]

Charity

But charity means pardoning what is unpardonable, or it is no virtue at all.

It is true that there is a thing crudely called charity, which means charity to the deserving poor; but charity to the deserving is not charity at all, but justice.

(H, ch. 12)

Stated baldly, charity certainly means one of two
things—pardoning unpardonable acts, or loving unlov-
able people.

(O, ch. 6)

Children; Youth

The fascination of children lies in this: that with
each of them all things are remade, and the universe is
put again upon its trial.

As we walk the streets and see below us those
delightful bulbous heads, three times too big for the body,
which mark these human mushrooms, we ought always
primarily to remember that within every one of these
heads there is a new universe, as new as it was on the
seventh day of creation.

Our attitude towards children consists in a conde-
scending indulgence, overlying an unfathomable respect.

(DEF, ch. 14)

It is the same with children; children are simply
human beings who are allowed to do what everyone else
really desires to do, as for instance, to fly kites, or when
seriously wronged to emit prolonged screams for several
minutes.

A child is a human being who has not grown up; to
hear educationists talk one would think he was some
variety of a deep-sea fish.

If we take children, for instance, as examples of the uncorrupted human animal, we see that the very things which appear in them in a manner primary and prominent, are the very things that philosophers have taught us to regard as sophisticated and over-civilized.

The instinct for a pompous intricate and recurring ceremonial, for instance, comes to a child like an organic hunger; he asks for a formality as he might ask for a drink of water.

(SL, "The Philosophy of Islands" [1903])

One of the profound philosophical truths which are almost confined to infants is this love of things, not for their use or origin, but for their own inherent characteristics, the child's love of the toughness of wood, the wetness of water, the magnificent soapiness of soap.

(TWE, ch. 12)

And in nothing is the child so righteously childlike, in nothing does he exhibit more accurately the sounder order of simplicity, than in the fact that he sees everything with a simple pleasure, even the complex things.

To the child the tree and the lamp-post are as natural and as artificial as each other; or rather, neither of them are natural but both supernatural.

(H, ch. 10)

A child is weaker than a man if it comes to a fight or to knowledge of the world; but there is nothing to show that the child is weaker in will or in desire.

(ILN, "Moral Education in a Secular World," 5-30-08)

If you keep bogies and goblins away from children they would make them up for themselves.

One small child can imagine monsters too big and black to get into any picture, and give them names too unearthly and cacophonous to have occurred in the cries of any lunatic.

The child, to begin with, commonly likes horrors, and he continues to indulge in them even when he does not like them.

(TRE, ch. 17)

Playing as children means playing is the most serious thing in the world; and as soon as we have small duties or small sorrows we have to abandon to some extent so enormous and ambitious a plan of life.

My journalistic work, which earns money, is not pursued with such awful persistency as that work which earned nothing.

The little girls that I meet in the little streets of Battersea worship their dolls in a way that reminds one not so much of play as idolatry.

(TRE, ch. 23)

Children who are lucky enough to be left alone in the nursery invent not only whole games, but whole dramas and life-stories of their own; they invent secret languages; they create imaginary families; they laboriously conduct family magazines.

(TT, ch. 35)

If anybody chooses to say that I have founded all my social philosophy on the antics of a baby, I am quite satisfied to bow and smile.

(ILN, "The Game of Self-Limitation," 2-8-30)

It is a dogma imposed on all, by the dogmatic secularism of the modern system, that Youth needs, must have, and cannot possibly be happy without, a riot of dances, plays, or entertainments.

And from what I remember of being young, and what I have read of the real reminiscences of youth, I incline to think that youth never shows its glorious vividness and vitality so much as when transfiguring what might be called monotony.

I can recall in my childhood the continuous excitement of long days in which nothing happened; and an indescribable sense of fullness in large and empty rooms.

Youth is much more capable of amusing itself than is now supposed, and in much less mortal need of being amused.

(ILN, "The Joy of Dullness," 5-3-30)

Why dreams are different from daylight, why dead things are different from live things, why he himself is different from others, why beauty makes us restless and even love is a spring of quarrels, why we cannot so fit into our environment as to forget it and ourselves; all these things are felt vaguely by children on long, empty afternoons; or by primitive poets writing the epics and legends of the morning of the world.

(AIS, ch. 25)

I think he instantly asserts his direct and divine right to enjoy beauty; that he steps straight into his own lawful kingdom of imagination, without any quibbles or questions such as arise afterwards out of false moralities and philosophies, touching the nature of falsehood and truth.

(CM, "The Pantomime")

[see also: Adventure, Fairy-Tales, Imagination, Mythology, Romanticism, Stories, Wonder]

Chivalry

It is a delicate balance between the sexes which gives the rarest and most poetic kind of pleasure to those who can strike it.

Wherever there is chivalry there is courtesy; and wherever there is courtesy there is comedy.

(NJ, ch. 2)

Chivalry is not the romantic, but the realistic, view of the sexes.

(TT, ch. 6)

[see also: Fairy Tales, Marriage, Middle Ages, Romanticism]

Christianity; Christendom

What has survived through an age of atheism as the most indestructible would survive through an age of polytheism as the most indispensable.

(NJ, ch. 8)

It met the mythological search for romance by being a story and the philosophical search for truth by being a true story.

(EM, II-5)

The fact is this: that the modern world, with its modern movements, is living on its Catholic capital.

(TT, ch. 3)

[see also: Authority (Religious), Catholicism & Catholics, Catholicity, Church (Catholic), Conversion (Catholic), Development (Doctrinal), Dogma (Catholic), History (Church), Orthodoxy, Paganism (and Christianity), Papacy & Popes, Protestantism, Reformation (Catholic), Religion (Organized), Theologians, Tradition]

Christmas

Christmas remains to remind us of those ages, whether Pagan or Christian, when the many acted poetry instead of the few writing it.

(H, ch. 6)

If Christmas could become more domestic, instead of less, I believe there would be a vast increase in the real Christmas spirit; the spirit of the Child.

Christmas is, as I have said, one of numberless old European feasts of which the essence is the combination of religion with merry-making.

For the character of Christmas (as distinct, for instance, from the continental Easter) lies chiefly in two things; first on the terrestrial side the note of comfort rather than the note of brightness; and on the spiritual side, Christian charity rather than Christian ecstasy.

(CD, ch. 7)

This is, first and last, the real value of Christmas; in so far as the mythology remains at all it is a kind of happy mythology.

Personally, of course, I believe in Santa Claus; but it is the season of forgiveness, and I will forgive others for not doing so.

(TRE, ch. 17)

Church, Catholic

I do believe in Christianity, and my impression is that a system must be divine which has survived so much insane mismanagement.

(ILN, "Superstition and Modern Justice," 10-6-06)

For, indeed, those who understand the Catholic tradition of Christianity are not offering a Church which is exclusively at issue with modern things, or even one that was exclusively expressed in mediaeval things.

The point is not so much that that age was relatively right while this age is relatively wrong; it is rather that the Church was relatively right when all ages were relatively wrong.

(ROC, Epilogue)

Surely anybody's commonsense would tell him that enthusiasts who only met through their common enthusiasm for a leader whom they loved, would not instantly rush away to establish everything that he hated.

If we trace it back to such very early Christians we must trace it back to Christ.

(EM, II-4)

And even a person who thinks it fortunate that the Church broke up into sects ought to be able to distinguish between the little things he likes and the big thing he has broken.

It is the Quaker meeting-house that is inside the Catholic cathedral; it is the Catholic cathedral that covers everything like the vault of the Crystal Palace; and it is when we look up at the vast distant dome covering all the exhibits that we trace the Gothic roof and the pointed windows.

The principle of life in all these variations of Protestantism, in so far as it is not a principle of death, consists of what remained in them of Catholic Christendom; and to Catholic Christendom they have always returned to be recharged with vitality.

(CCC, ch. 4)

The Catholic Church is the only thing which saves a man from the degrading slavery of being a child of his age.

A thing as old as the Catholic Church has an accumulated armoury and treasury to choose from; it can pick and choose among the centuries and brings one age to the rescue of another.

(CCC, ch. 5)

First it must be remembered that the Church is always in advance of the world.

(WEL, "The Case of Spain")

[see also: Agnosticism, Authority (Religious), Catholicism & Catholics, Catholicity, Christianity, Conversion (Catholic), Development (Doctrinal), Dogma (Catholic), History & Historians, History (Church), Orthodoxy, Paganism (and Christianity), Papacy & Popes, Protestantism, Reformation (Catholic), Religion (Organized), Skepticism, Theologians, Tradition]

Cities

If whenever I tried to walk down the road I found the whole thoroughfare one crawling carpet of spiders, closely interlocked, I should feel a distress verging on distaste.

It is not humanity that disgusts us in the huge cities; it is inhumanity.

It is not that there are human beings; but that they are not treated as such.

We do not, I hope, dislike men and women; we only dislike their being made into a sort of jam: crushed together
so that they are not merely powerless but shapeless.

I do not want the nearest human house to be too distant to see; that is my objection to the wilderness.

But neither do I want the nearest human house to be
too close to see; that is my objection to the modern city.

I love my fellow-man; I do not want him so far off
that I can only observe anything of him through a telescope, nor do I want him so close that I can examine parts
of him with a microscope.

I want him within a stone's throw of me; so that
whenever it is really necessary, I may throw the stone.

(AD, ch. 21)

A traveller sees the hundred branches of a tree long
before he is near enough to see its single and simple root;
he generally sees the scattered or sprawling suburbs of
a town long before he has looked upon the temple or the
market-place.

(NJ, ch. 7)

They have built a city of houses only notable for
the size of the ground-rent and the smallness of the
ground-plan; a city of whose wealth and poverty they
are alike ashamed; a city from which they themselves
flee into the country, and which they themselves cannot prevent from crawling outwards into the country to
pursue them.

(ROC, Epilogue)

[see also: Architecture, Automobiles, Capitalism, Communications, Hustle & Bustle, Inventions, Traffic]

Cleanliness

For my part, I think brightness more important than cleanliness; since the first is of the soul, and the second of the body.

(TRE, ch. 37)

As if everyone did not know that while saints can afford to be dirty, seducers have to be clean.

 As if everyone did not know that the harlot must be clean, because it is her business to captivate, while the good wife may be dirty, because it is her business to clean.

As if we did not all know that whenever God's thunder cracks above us, it is very likely indeed to find the simplest man in a muck cart and the most complex blackguard in a bath.

(WWW, IV-11)

I am even ready to admit that cleanliness is next to godliness; but the moderns will not even admit godliness to be next to cleanliness.

(WWW, "Three Notes," II)

Cliques

There is nothing really narrow about the clan; the thing which is really narrow is the clique.

But the men of the clique live together because they have the same kind of soul, and their narrowness is a narrowness of spiritual coherence and contentment, like that which exists in hell.

(H, ch. 14)

This is the paradox of the clique; that it consists of those who understand something and do not wish it to be understood; do not really wish it to be understandable.

(AIS, ch. 18)

[see also: Conversation, Friendship, Neighbors, Silent Types, Singing, Talkers]

Common Sense

And the first fact of common sense is the common bond of men.

(NJ, ch. 2)

Indeed, we might say that when men boast of common-sense, it generally means a contempt for common people.

(ILN, "Spiritualism and Agnosticism," 1-12-29)

It is so easy to say something to start with that sounds splendidly sensible, and so difficult afterwards to reconcile it with common sense.

(ILN, "The Modern Recoil From the Modern," 11-9-29)

It might have taken the world a long time to understand that what it had been taught to dismiss as mediaeval theology was often mere common sense; although the very term common sense, or *communis sententia*, was a mediaeval conception.

But it took the world very little time to understand that the talk on the other side was most uncommon nonsense.

(WEL, "The Return to Religion")

[see also: Critics, Experts, Gentlemen, "Higher Culture," Humanitarianism, Intelligentsia, Man (Common), Prigs]

Communications, Modern

Civilisation is not to be judged by the rapidity of communication, but by the value of what is communicated.

(ILN, "America and Barbarism," 2-16-07)

[see also: Automobiles, Capitalism, Cities, Hustle & Bustle, Inventions, Traffic]

Compartmentalization

The whole is one vast system of separation – an enormous philosophical Divorce Court.

This endless process of separation of everything from everything else has a good example, for instance, in the case of religion.

Religion, a human and historic religion, like Christianity or Buddhism or some great periods of Paganism was, as a matter of fact, a combination of all the important parts of life.

Every one of the main human interests was in old times made a part of the creed.

Every one of those human interests is now put apart by itself, as if it were a monomania like collecting stamps.
(SL, "On Fragments" [1906])

Now it is the great mark of our modernity that people are always proposing substitutes for these old things; and these substitutes always answer one purpose where the old thing answered ten.

But I do not think the most austere upholder of specialism will deny that there is in these old, many-sided institutions an element of unity and universality which may well be preserved in its due proportion and place.

Spiritually, at least, it will be admitted that some all-round balance is needed to equalize the extravagance of experts.

Everything has been sundered from everything else, and everything has grown cold.

What makes it difficult for the average man to be a universalist is that the average man has to be a specialist; he has not only to learn one trade, but to learn it so well as to uphold him in a more or less ruthless society.
(WWW, III-2)

[see also: Anthropology, Ceremony, Customs, Environment, Man, Man (Smallness of), Nationality, Sociology]

Compassion

A great man is not a man so strong that he feels less than other men; he is a man so strong that he feels more.

(H, ch. 5)

Confession

I do not know anything about psycho-analysis, except that it demands a great deal more than the Confessional was always abused for demanding.

(ILN, "Dr. Freud and Ancient Myth," 10-26-29)

And to their nightmare fancy a confessional box is a sort of man-trap; and presents in its very appearance some combination of a coffin and a cage.

(WEL, "The Church and Agoraphobia")

Well, when a Catholic comes from Confession, he does truly, by definition, step out again into that dawn of his own beginning and look with new eyes across the world to a Crystal Palace that is really of crystal.

(A, ch. 16)

[see also: Asceticism, Faith, Incense, Martyrdom, Mysticism, Relics, Robes, Sabbath, Temptation]

Conformity; Herd Mentality

The minds of men are not so much alike as the motor-cars of men, or the morning papers of men, or the mechanical manufacture of the coats and hats of men.

Just as we spread paving-stones over different soils without reference to the different crops that might grow there, so we spread programmes of platitudinous plutocracy over souls that God made various, and simpler societies have made free.

(OS, ch. 4)

If we want character, in the old unique sense of being "a character," we are much more likely to find it in Christians who accepted the Imitation of Christ than in all these millions of materialists who are taught to imitate each other.

(ILN, "Personality in the Modern World," 2-25-28)

In any case, my own experience of the modern world tells me that Catholics are much more and not less individualistic than other men in their general opinions.

(TT, ch. 22)

[see also: Fashions, Nonconformity (Christian), Spirit of the Age (*Zeitgeist*)]

Conscience

It is worth noting in connection with conversion, because the convert is often obstructed by a catchword which says that the Church crushes the conscience.

It is the man who crushes his conscience and then finds out that it was right, when he has almost forgotten that he had one.

(CCC, ch. 5)

Conservatism

Revolutionists make a reform, Conservatives only conserve the reform.

They never reform the reform, which is often very much wanted.

(WWW, IV-12)

The sort of snob who sneers at poverty commonly calls himself a Conservative.

(ILN, "Certain Incongruities at Christmas," 12-22-23)

I suppose most conservatives are conserving the tradition of the last revolt.

(ILN, "Original Sin and the Moderns," 9-1-28)

[see also: Anarchy, Aristocracy, Caesaropapism, Democracy, Government, Law, Liberalism (Political), Monarchy, Nationalism, Nazism, Patriotism, Politicians, Revolution, Socialism, Spain (Civil War), Tolerance, Voting]

Conspiratorialism

If a man says (for instance) that men have a conspiracy against him, you cannot dispute it except by saying that all the men deny that they are conspirators; which is exactly what conspirators would do.

(O, ch. 2)

[see also: Bigotry & Racism, Broadmindedness, Dogmatism, Madness, Openmindedness, Prejudice, Tolerance]

Contraception

Some say that the poor should give up having children, which means that they should give up their great virtue of sexual sanity.

(CD, ch. 7)

People would understand better the popular fury against the witches, if they remembered that the malice most commonly attributed to them was preventing the birth of children.

(EM, I-6)

I might inform those humanitarians who have a nightmare of new and needless babies (for some humanitarians have that sort of horror of humanity) that if the recent decline in the birth-rate were continued for a certain time, it might end in there being no babies at all; which would console them very much.

(ILN, "The Place of Mysticism," 5-24-30)

Perhaps the nearest to a description of it is to say this: that my contempt boils over into bad behaviour when I hear the common suggestion that a birth is avoided because people want to be "free" to go to the cinema or buy a gramophone or a loud-speaker.

(WEL, "Babies and Distributism")

It has been left to the last Christians, or rather to the first Christians fully committed to blaspheming and denying Christianity, to invent a new kind of worship of Sex, which is not even a worship of Life.

It has been left to the very latest Modernists to proclaim an erotic religion which at once exalts lust and forbids fertility.

The new priests abolish the fatherhood and keep the feast to themselves.

(WEL, "Sex and Property")

[see also: Abortion, Abstinence, Birth Control, Eugenics, Euphemisms, Euthanasia, Family, Feminism, Home, Motherhood, Sexuality]

Conversation

In order to have, like Dr. Johnson, a good talk, it is emphatically necessary to be, like Dr. Johnson, a good man—to have friendship and honour and an abysmal tenderness.

Above all, it is necessary to be openly and indecently humane, to confess with fullness all the primary pities and fears of Adam.

(H, ch. 15)

People talking in twos talk gently, because they feel emphatically: people talking in tens or twenties talk emphatically because they do not care a dump about anything.

It is true; men do speak to a motion, not about it; they talk to a topic.

Women talk to each other; that is why their conversations are frightfully fascinating, but too terrible for us to listen to for long without running away.

Our sex is not strong or bold enough to endure that agony of directly personal conversation in which women are supreme.

We must have a topic—an impersonal one.
(AWD, "A Case of Comrades" [1908])

If the pleasure-seeker himself were really a pleasure-maker for himself, if he were forced to amuse himself instead of being amused, if he were, in short, obliged to sit down in an old tavern and talk—I am really very doubtful about whether he would confine his conversation entirely to the Crown Prince of Fontarabia, the shingling of hair, the greatness of certain rich Yankees, and so on; and then begin the same round of subjects all over again.
(OS, ch. 4)

[see also: Cliques, Friendship, Neighbors, Silent Types, Singing, Talkers]

Conversion and Converts (Catholic)

The Church is a house with a hundred gates; and no two men enter at exactly the same angle.

But it is not really a question of what a man is made to believe but of what he must believe; what he cannot help believing.

He cannot disbelieve in an elephant when he has seen one; and he cannot treat the Church as a child when he has discovered that she is his mother.
(CCC, ch. 2)

When a man really sees the Church, even if he dislikes what he sees, he does not see what he had expected to dislike.

Nobody has any notion of what the whole story is about, who does not know that, through those long and dark and indecisive days, it is the man who persecutes himself.

I had no more idea of becoming a Catholic than of becoming a cannibal.

The second stage is that in which the convert begins to be conscious not only of the falsehood but the truth and is enormously excited to find that there is far more of it than he would ever have expected.

It is like discovering a new continent full of strange flowers and fantastic animals, which is at once wild and hospitable.

It is, broadly speaking, the stage in which the man is unconsciously trying to be converted.

The moment men cease to pull against it they feel a tug towards it.

The moment they try to be fair to it they begin to be fond of it.

If I may refer once more to a personal experience, I may say that I for one was never less troubled by doubts than in the last phase, when I was troubled by fears.

And by a paradox that does not frighten me now in the least, it may be that I shall never again have such absolute assurance that the thing is true as I had when I made my last effort to deny it.

Becoming a Catholic broadens the mind.

Only, when he has entered the Church, he finds that the Church is much larger inside than it is outside.

(CCC, ch. 3)

To become a Catholic is not to leave off thinking, but to learn how to think.

Nothing is more amusing to the convert, when his conversion has been complete for some time, than to hear the speculations about when or whether he will repent of the conversion; when he will be sick of it, how long he will stand it, at what stage of his external exasperation he will start up and say he can bear it no more.

(CCC, ch. 4)

[see also: Authority (Religious), Catholicism & Catholics, Catholicity, Christianity, Church (Catholic), Development (Doctrinal), Dogma (Catholic), History (Church), Orthodoxy, Paganism (and Christianity), Papacy & Popes, Protestantism, Reformation (Catholic), Religion (Organized), Theologians]

Courage

It means a strong desire to live taking the form of a readiness to die.

(O, ch. 6)

Creation

Nobody can imagine how nothing could turn into something.

(EM, I-1)

In fact, about the nearest approach to the very latest speculations of the physicists is the ancient formula that it was out of Nothing that God made the world.

(ILN, "Religion and the New Science," 4-12-30)

[see also: Darwinism, Life (Origin of), Materialism, Medicine (Alternative), Nature, Pantheism, Physics (Modern), Science, Science (and Religion), Theism, Wonder]

Critics

Shakespeare is quite himself; it is only some of his critics who have discovered that he was somebody else.

(O, ch. 2)

They are separated by a great chasm of "culture" and fastidiousness from the people for whom they write.

As men they should laugh or cry at a theatre; and then afterwards, as critics, defend themselves for having done so.

They should justify to the public its own feelings in the act of justifying their own.

(ILN, "Politicians and Their Constitutions," 11-20-09)

What is wrong with the critic is that he does not criticise himself.

(NJ, ch. 4)

Most critics do not see the facts at all.

(ILN, "England and Dogmatic Christianity," 2-9-29)

That is also, as it happens, exactly what Mr. Chesterton said, and all that Mr. Chesterton said; and Mr. Chesterton is very much gratified to learn that it is also what he ought to have said.

(WEL, "Frozen Free Thought")

[see also: Common Sense, Experts, Gentlemen, "Higher Culture," Humanitarianism, Intelligentsia, Man (Common), Prigs]

Cro-Magnon Man

It is an insult to the professors sitting round the dinner-table to suggest that there were ever any heads bigger than their own.

(ILN, "Outlines of History," 1-13-23)

[see also: Creation, Darwinism, Life (Origin of), Materialism, Medicine (Alternative), Physics (Modern), Science, Science (and Religion)]

Cross, The; Crucifixes

But the cross, though it has at its heart a collision and a contradiction, can extend its four arms for ever without altering its shape.

(O, ch. 2)

The Greek cross is a cross; the Roman cross is a crucifix.

(NJ, ch. 5)

It is true, and even tautological, to say that the cross is the crux of the whole matter.

(EM, I-6)

[see also: Angels, Death, Evil, Ghosts, Incarnation, Jesus, Mary, Mass, Miracles, Original Sin, Resurrection, Sacramentalism, Saints, Satan & Demons, Sin, Transubstantiation, Trinitarianism]

Crusades, The

For instance, the Crusades ended in the defeat of the Christians.

But they did not end in the decline of the Christians; they ended in the decline of the Saracens.

That huge prophetic wave of Moslem power which had hung in the very heavens above the towns of Christendom, that wave was broken, and never came on again.

(TRE, ch. 20)

The Americans said, and perhaps thought, that they were fighting for democracy; and the Crusaders said, and perhaps thought, that they were fighting for Christianity.

But as we know what the Crusaders meant better than they did themselves, I cannot quite understand why we do not enjoy the same valuable omniscience about the Americans.

The Crusade was a religious movement, but it was also a perfectly rational movement; one might almost say a rationalist movement.

But it certainly is the fact that religious war is in itself much more rational than patriotic war.

But it cannot be denied that there is more of mere passion, of mere preference and prejudice, in short of mere personal accident, in fighting another nation than in fighting another faith.

The Crusader is in every sense more rational than the modern conscript or professional soldier.

He is more rational in his object, which is the intelligent and intelligible object of conversion; where the modern militarist has an object much more confused by momentary vanity and one-sided satisfaction.

The object of all war is peace; but the object of religious war is mental as well as material peace; it is agreement.

In short religious war aims ultimately at equality, where national war aims relatively at superiority.

In that sense alone it is foolish for us in the West to sneer at those who kill men when a foot is set in a holy place, when we ourselves kill hundreds of thousands when a foot is put across a frontier.

It is absurd for us to despise those who shed blood for a relic when we have shed rivers of blood for a rag.

But above all the Crusade, or, for that matter, the Jehad, is by far the most philosophical sort of fighting, not only in its conception of ending the difference, but in its mere act of recognising the difference, as the deepest kind of difference.

It is to reverse all reason to suggest that a man's politics matter and his religion does not matter.

Christendom would have been entirely justified in the abstract in being alarmed or suspicious at the mere rise of a great power that was not Christian.

The critic of the Crusade talks as if it had sought out some inoffensive tribe or temple in the interior of Thibet, which was never discovered until it was invaded.

They seem entirely to forget that long before the Crusaders had dreamed of riding to Jerusalem, the Moslems had almost ridden into Paris.

They seem to forget that if the Crusaders nearly conquered Palestine, it was but a return upon the Moslems who had nearly conquered Europe.

The Crusade was the counter-attack.

It was the defensive army taking the offensive in its turn, and driving back the enemy to his base.

In order to understand this religious war we must class it, not so much with the wars of history as with the revolutions of history.

As I shall try to show briefly on a later page, it not only had all the peculiar good and the peculiar evil of things like the French Revolution or the Russian Revolution, but it was a more purely popular revolution than either of them.

It was not only essentially a revolution, but it was the only revolution I know of in which the masses began by acting alone, and practically without any support from any of the classes.

(NJ, ch. 11)

In these medieval pilgrims every inconsistency is a hypocrisy; while in the more modern patriots even an infamy is only an inconsistency.

(NJ, ch. 12)

[see also: "Dark Ages," Empires, Greeks, History, History (Church), Hypocrisy (of Christians), Inquisition, Middle Ages, Renaissance, Tolerance, Victorianism, War, War (and Christianity)]

Customs

No; the aristocrats never have customs; at the best they have habits, like the animals.

Only the mob has customs.

(WWW, I-10)

[see also: Anthropology, Ceremony, Compartmentalization, Environment, Man, Man (Smallness of), Nationality, Sociology]

Dancing

But if he had ever felt himself the ancient, sublime, elemental, human instinct to dance, he would have discovered that dancing is not a frivolous thing at all, but a very serious thing.

I should regard any civilization which was without a universal habit of uproarious dancing as being, from the full human point of view, a defective civilization.

(H, ch. 16)

I do not say that I think most of the modern dancing I see is anything likely to be a diabolic distraction from the beatific vision; but that is a matter of particular taste and passing fashion.

Pure and absolute beauty is attainable by dancing, if not always attained by dancers.

(ILN, "About Means and Ends," 12-11-26)

0

"Dark Ages"

And in history I found that Christianity, so far from belonging to the Dark Ages, was the one path across the Dark Ages that was not dark.

(O, ch. 9)

Because I deny the universal generalization that the Dark Ages were dark, he argues that I must be denying that the Black Death was black.

(ILN, "Mediaeval Robber Barons and Other Myths," 5-26-23)

Certainly there were Dark Ages following on the decline of the old pagan civilization; but it is quite the reverse of self-evident that it was through religion that the civilization declined.

They assume that Danish pirates would all have wanted to join Ethical Societies and attend University Extension lectures, but for deplorable obstacles like St. Dunstan.

It is suggested that Border chieftains would all have been arguing in debating clubs about evolution and ethics, but for the blighting influence of theology.

(ILN, "Modern Doubts and Questioning," 2-13-26)

He imagines that the Danish pirate was talking about Tariff Reform and Imperial Preference, with scientific statistics from Australia and Alaska, when he was rudely interrupted by a monk named Bede, who had never heard of anything but monkish fables.

He supposes that a Viking or a Visigoth was firmly founded on the principles of the Primrose League and the English Speaking Union, and that everything else would have been founded on them if fanatical priests had not rushed in and proclaimed the savage cult called Christianity.

(TT, ch. 14)

[see also: Crusades, Empires, Greeks, History, History (Church), Hypocrisy (of Christians), Inquisition, Middle Ages, Renaissance, Tolerance, Victorianism, War, War (and Christianity)]

Darwinism and Evolution

If evolution simply means that a positive thing called an ape turned very slowly into a positive thing called a man, then it is stingless for the most orthodox; for a personal God might just as well do things slowly as quickly, especially if, like the Christian God, he were outside time.

(O, ch. 3)

Darwinism can be used to back up two mad moralities, but it cannot be used to back up a single sane one.

(O, ch. 7)

Or it is as if I were told that I liked to swim in the sea, solely because some early forms of amphibian life came out of the sea on to the shore.

I answer that I know why I swim in the sea; and it is because the divine gift of reason tells me that it would be unsatisfactory to swim on the land.

(NJ, ch. 11)

It is a mark of the credulity of Victorian rationalism that the rationalist did so easily become a Darwinian.

Claiming to have cast off the superstitions of others, it contrives with astonishing rapidity to create superstitions of its own; as is here shown in the very short period that has turned Charles Darwin from an honest man into an unhuman god.

(ILN, "Mr. Archer's Defense of Darwinism," 12-8-23)

Apparently it is not cheek to say you have lost faith in Deity or immortality, but it is cheek to say you have lost faith in Darwin.

(ILN, "Modern Doubts and Questioning," 2-13-26)

[see also: Creation, Life (Origin of), Materialism, Medicine (Alternative), Physics (Modern), Science, Science (and Religion), Theism]

Death

Again, the educated classes have adopted a hideous and heathen custom of considering death as too dreadful to talk about, and letting it remain a secret for each person, like some private malformation.

The poor, on the contrary, make a great gossip and display about bereavement; and they are right.

They have hold of a truth of psychology which is at the back of all the funeral customs of the children of men.

The way to lessen sorrow is to make a lot of it.

(WWW, IV-13)

[see also: Angels, Cross, Evil, Ghosts, Incarnation, Jesus, Mary, Mass, Miracles, Original Sin, Resurrection, Sacramentalism, Saints, Satan & Demons, Sin, Transubstantiation, Trinitarianism]

Decadence

That is the whole essence of decadence, the effacement of five people who do a thing for fun by one person who does it for money.

(H, ch. 16)

Democracy; Equality

If a man is genuinely superior to his fellows the first thing that he believes in is the equality of man.

To very great minds the things on which men agree are so immeasurably more important than the things on which they differ, that the latter, for all practical purposes, disappear.

(H, ch. 17)

Democracy is not founded on pity for the common man; democracy is founded on reverence for the common man, or, if you will, even on fear of him.

It is a certain instinctive attitude which feels the things in which all men agree to be unspeakably important, and all the things in which they differ (such as mere brains) to be almost unspeakably unimportant.

It is a sufficient proof that we are not an essentially democratic state that we are always wondering what we shall do with the poor.

If we were democrats, we should be wondering what the poor will do with us.

A purely democratic state perhaps there has never been.
(H, ch. 19)

But even the machinery of voting is profoundly Christian in this practical sense—that it is an attempt to get at the opinion of those who would be too modest to offer it.
(O, ch. 7)

It cannot be too often repeated that all real democracy is an attempt (like that of a jolly hostess) to bring the shy people out.

Democracy means getting those people to vote who would never have the cheek to govern: and (according to Christian ethics) the precise people who ought to govern are the people who have not the cheek to do it.
(TRE, ch. 32)

You must excuse me; I am a democrat; I know I am out of fashion in the modern world.
(TRE, ch. 37)

But representative government, the one universal relic, is a very poor fragment of the full republican idea.
(WWW, I-5)

The sceptic ultimately undermines democracy (1) because he can see no significance in death and such things of a literal equality; (2) because he introduces different first principles, making debate impossible: and debate is the life of democracy; (3) because the fading of the images of sacred persons leaves a man too prone to be a respecter of earthly persons; (4) because there will be more, not less, respect for human rights if they can be treated as divine rights.

(ILN, "Mystical Belief and Popular Government," 1-13-12)

The modern industrial world is not in the least democratic; but it is supposed to be democratic, or supposed to be trying to be democratic.

And democracy is the only ideal the industrial millions have, when they have any at all.

It is this which prophets promise to achieve, and politicians pretend to achieve, and poets sometimes desire to achieve, and sometimes only desire to desire.

In a word, an equal citizenship is quite the reverse of the reality in the modern world; but it is still the ideal in the modern world.

(NJ, ch. 1)

He who believes in the existence of God believes in the equality of man.

(NJ, ch. 2)

People are entitled to self-government; that is, to such government as is self-made.

It is their right to make it for themselves, but it is also their duty to think of it for themselves.

(NJ, ch. 5)

Anyhow, peasants tilling patches of their own land in a rough equality, and meeting to vote directly under a village tree, are the most truly self-governing of men.

(EM, I-3)

The old morality, the Christian religion, the Catholic Church, differed from all this new mentality because it really believed in the rights of men.

That is, it believed that ordinary men were clothed with powers and privileges and a kind of authority.

(OS, ch. 6)

Democracy is a very noble thing, and it does not exist – at any rate at present.

(ILN, "Quackery About the Family," 7-12-30)

[see also: Anarchy, Aristocracy, Caesaropapism, Conservatism, Government, Law, Liberalism (Political), Monarchy, Nationalism, Nazism, Patriotism, Politicians, Revolution, Socialism, Spain (Civil War), Tolerance, Voting]

Despair

Despair does not lie in being weary of suffering, but in being weary of joy.

(EM, I-8)

[see also: Fanatics, Madness, Moods, Optimism, Pessimism, Resignation, Suicide]

Determinism

It is absurd to say that you are especially advancing freedom when you only use free thought to destroy free will.

The determinist makes the theory of causation quite clear, and then finds that he cannot say "if you please" to the housemaid.

(O, ch. 2)

[see also: Agnosticism, Atheism, Darwinism, Materialism, Modernism, Physics (Modern), Science, Secularism, Skepticism]

Development, Doctrinal

When we say that a puppy develops into a dog, we do not mean that his growth is a gradual compromise with a cat; we mean that he becomes more doggy and not less.

Development is the expansion of all the possibilities and implications of a doctrine, as there is time to distinguish them and draw them out; and the point here is that the enlargement of medieval theology was simply the full comprehension of that theology.

The Thomist movement in metaphysics, like the Franciscan movement in morals and manners, was an enlargement and a liberation, it was emphatically a growth of Christian theology from within; it was emphatically *not* a shrinking of Christian theology under heathen or even human influences.

Nobody can understand the greatness of the thirteenth century, who does not realise that it was a great growth of new things produced by a living thing.

(STA, ch. 1)

[see also: Authority (Religious), Catholicism & Catholics, Catholicity, Christianity, Church (Catholic), Conversion (Catholic), Dogma (Catholic), History (Church), Orthodoxy, Paganism (and Christianity), Papacy & Popes, Protestantism, Reformation (Catholic), Religion (Organized), Theologians, Tradition]

Distributism; Property

When you have discovered why enormous English estates were not long ago cut up into small holdings like the land of France, you will have discovered why the Englishman is more drunken than the Frenchman.

(TRE, ch. 12)

Property is merely the art of the democracy.

It means that every man should have something that he can shape in his own image, as he is shaped in the image of heaven.

(WWW, I-6)

Whether we can give every English man a free home of his own or not, at least we should desire it; and he desires it.

To give nearly everybody ordinary houses would please nearly everybody; that is what I assert without apology.

(WWW, I-8)

The idea of private property universal but private, the idea of families free but still families, of domesticity democratic but still domestic, of one man one house—this remains the real vision and magnet of mankind.

(WWW, I-11)

If we want property to be a part of the commonwealth we must make it common, not in the sense of a communal ownership, but in the sense of a common experience.

(ILN, "Capitalism and Real Ownership," 3-31-23)

What is wrong is not that there is one class of property, but that there is another class without property.

What is wrong is that this class without property has to hire itself out to the propertied class in order to live at all.

(ILN, "Eliminating the Class Without Property," 11-8-24)

About fifteen years ago a few of us began to preach, in the old *New Age and New Witness*, a policy of small

distributed property (which has since assumed the awk-
ward but accurate name of Distributism), as we should
have said then, against the two extremes of Capitalism
and Communism.

The theory that those who start reasonably equal
cannot remain reasonably equal is a fallacy founded
entirely on a society in which they start extremely
unequal.

It is our whole point that the central power needs
lesser powers to balance and check it, and that these
must be of many kinds: some individual, some communal, some official, and so on.

(OS, ch. 1)

But as I happen to like seeing a free man own a free
field, or a human being doing something with his own
head and hand, I do not think that the tendency towards
Trusts is the tendency towards Truth.

(ILN, "Criticism of the Creeds," 1-28-28)

The complexity of commercial society has become
intolerable, because that society is commercial and nothing else.

I mean that the actual direct and isolated enjoyment of private property, as distinct from the excitement
of exchanging it or getting a profit on it, is rather rarer
than in many simple communities that seem almost communal in their simplicity.

(WEL, "Reflections on a Rotten Apple")

Now the notion of narrowing property merely to enjoying money is exactly like the notion of narrowing love merely to enjoying sex.

(WEL, "Sex and Property")

[see also: Capitalism, Guilds, Philanthropy, Poor, Publicity, Simplicity, Socialism, Thrift, Wealth]

Divorce

If married people are to be divorced for incompatibility of temper, I cannot imagine why all married people are not divorced.

(ILN, "Incompatibility in Marriage," 9-19-08)

To complain that I could only be married once was like complaining that I had only been born once.

(O, ch. 4)

Even in order to be divorced it has generally been found necessary to go through the preliminary formality of being married; and unless the nature of this initial act be considered, we might as well be discussing haircutting for the bald or spectacles for the blind.

To be divorced is to be in the literal sense unmarried; and there is no sense in a thing being undone when we do not know if it is done.

(SD, ch. 1)

While free love seems to me a heresy, divorce does really seem to me a superstition.

It is not only more of a superstition than free love, but much more of a superstition than strict sacramental marriage; and this point can hardly be made too plain.

It is the partisans of divorce, not the defenders of marriage, who attach a stiff and senseless sanctity to a mere ceremony, apart from the meaning of the ceremony.

It is they who hold that vow or violation, loyalty or disloyalty, can all be disposed of by a mysterious and magic rite, performed first in a law-court and then in a church or a registry office.

We are talking about the idea of loyalty; perhaps a fantastic, perhaps only an unfashionable idea, but one we can explain and defend as an idea.

Now I have already pointed out that most sane men do admit our ideal in such a case as patriotism or public spirit; the necessity of saving the state to which we belong.

In short, everybody recognises that there is some ship, large and small, which he ought not to leave, even when he thinks it is sinking.

(SD, ch. 2)

So the unfortunate man, who cannot tolerate the woman he has chosen from all the women in the world, is not encouraged to return to her and tolerate her, but encouraged to choose another woman whom he may in due course refuse to tolerate.

(SD, ch. 4)

The child is an explanation of the father and mother and the fact that it is a human child is the explanation of the ancient human ties connecting the father and mother.

(SD, ch. 5)

The modern man wants to eat his wedding cake and have it, too.

But the broad-minded are extremely bitter because a Christian who wishes to have several wives when his own promise bound him to one, is not allowed to violate his vow at the same altar at which he made it.

Any man in modern London may have a hundred wives if he does not call them wives; or rather, if he does not go through certain more or less mystical ceremonies in order to assert that they are wives.

The definition of divorce, which concerns us here, is that it is the attempt to give respectability, and not liberty.

But the peculiar point here is that many are claiming the sanction of religion as well as of respectability.

They would attach to their very natural and sometimes very pardonable experiments a certain atmosphere, and even glamour, which has undoubtedly belonged to the status of marriage in historic Christendom.

People were regarded as having a certain dignity because they were dedicated in a certain way; as bound to certain duties and, if it be preferred, to certain discomforts.

But it is certainly much more irrational to respect them, and then artificially transfer the same respect to the absence of them.

But if we are really to dismiss our dreams of dignity and honour, if we are really to fall back on the frank realism of our experience as men of the world, then the very first thing that our experience will tell us is that it very seldom is a separation by mutual consent; that is, that the consent very seldom is sincerely and spontaneously mutual.

But the truth is that the innovators have as much sham optimism about divorce as any romanticist can have had about marriage.

They regard their story, when it ends in the divorce court, through as rosy a mist of sentimentalism as anybody ever regarded a story ending with wedding bells.

Such a reformer is quite sure that when once the prince and princess are divorced by the fairy godmother, they will live happily ever after.

I enjoy romance, but I like it to be rooted in reality; and any one with a touch of reality knows that nine couples out of ten, when they are divorced, are left in an exceedingly different state.

I say this in passing, to point out that while I do not dream of suggesting that there are only happy marriages, there will quite certainly, as things work nowadays, be a very large number of unhappy and unjust divorces.

It is a controversy about re-marriage; or rather about whether it is marriage at all.

(SD, ch. 7)

A man has only to commit the crime of desertion to obtain the reward of divorce.

And if they are entitled to take as typical the most horrible hypothetical cases of the abuse of the marriage laws, surely we are entitled to take equally extreme possibilities in the abuse of their own divorce laws.

The point of divorce reform, it cannot be too often repeated, is that the rascal should not only be regarded as romantic, but regarded as respectable.

He is not to sow his wild oats and settle down; he is merely to settle down to sowing his wild oats.

They must surely see that in England at present, as in many parts of America in the past, the new liberty is being taken in the spirit of licence as if the exception were to be the rule, or, rather, perhaps the absence of rule.

The obvious effect of frivolous divorce will be frivolous marriage.

If people can be separated for no reason they will feel it all the easier to be united for no reason.

A man might quite clearly foresee that a sensual infatuation would be fleeting, and console himself with the knowledge that the connection could be equally fleeting.

Instead of the old social distinction between those who are married and those who are unmarried, there will be a distinction between those who are married and those who are really married.

(SD, ch. 8)

But the point of divorce is not that people are professing to be reckless, but that people are pretending to be respectable. /

(ILN, "The Family of the Bright Young Things," 10-5-29)

How can a poor father get any real fun out of being divorced if his enjoyment is to be dashed by a morbid memory of the existence of his own son?

Similarly, if the new social philosophies fervently encouraged people to think more about domesticity and less about divorce, I might believe that they really were preferring the future generation to their own.

(ILN, "Living For the Future," 5-31-30)

Numbers of normal people are getting married, thinking already that they may be divorced.

The Church was right to refuse even the exception.

The world has admitted the exception; and the exception has become the rule.

But these people propose this easy method, in the hope that some people will only use it to a moderate extent; whereas it is much more probable that an indefinite number will use it to an indefinite extent.

(WEL, "The Surrender Upon Sex")

[see also: Family, Feminism, Fidelity, Gender Differences, Home, Marriage, Mothers-in-Law, Sexuality, Wives]

Dogma (Catholic)

Catholic doctrine and discipline may be walls; but they are the walls of a playground.

(O, ch. 9)

What the denouncer of dogma really means is not that dogma is bad; but rather that dogma is too good to be true.

(EM, II-5)

[see also: Authority (Religious), Catholicism & Catholics, Catholicity, Christianity, Church (Catholic), Conversion (Catholic), Development (Doctrinal), History (Church), Orthodoxy, Paganism (and Christianity), Papacy & Popes, Protestantism, Reformation (Catholic), Religion (Organized), Theologians, Tradition]

Dogmatism

The modern world is filled with men who hold dogmas so strongly that they do not even know that they are dogmas.

(H, ch. 20)

For the modern world will accept no dogmas upon any authority; but it will accept any dogmas on no authority.

(SD, ch. 5)

In other words, this world of to-day does not know that all the novels and newspapers that it reads or writes are in fact full of certain assumptions, that are just as dogmatic as dogmas.

(TT, ch. 15)

It is still supposed by many to be old-fashioned to dogmatise about dogmatic things, such as dogmas; but the new fashion is to dogmatise about undogmatic things, about mere likes and dislikes, about things that cannot be stated as dogmas even by the dogmatists.

(ILN, "The Only Rational Wars," 9-26-31)

[see also: Bigotry & Racism, Broadmindedness, Conspiratorialism, Liberalism (Political), Modernism, Openmindedness, Prejudice, Skepticism, Tolerance]

Dreams

The fact about dreams which is most interesting to our spiritual nature is this: that in our dreams we do recognise the existence of the identity of something quite apart from any of the facts by which we know it.

In short, the phenomena of dreams very strongly support, so far as they go, the old mystical doctrine that an absolute identity of things exists behind the visible world.

In dreams we are all Platonists.

(ILN, "The Psychology of Dreams," 4-6-07)

Education; Secular State Schools

The one thing that is never taught by any chance in the atmosphere of public schools is exactly that – that there is a whole truth of things, and that in knowing it and speaking it we are happy.

(ILN, "The Disappearing Middle Class," 8-11-06)

That is to say, the more doubtful we are about whether we have any truth, the more certain we are (apparently) that we can teach it to children.

I am quite prepared to promise the Secularists secular education, if they on their side will promise (on the tombs of their mothers) not to have moral instruction.

Teaching moral instruction means teaching modern London, Birmingham, and Boston ethics, which are not barbaric and rudimentary, but are corrupt, hysterical, and crawling with worms, and which are to a Christian, not unsatisfying, but detestable.

There is no education that is not sectarian education.

If I offer to teach a child without indicating in any way what sort of thing I mean to teach him, I am simply unintelligible.

(ILN, "Talking About Education," 1-26-07)

Many eminent men who have been quite rational about other things have been quite mad about education.

Men do not go mad by mobs, but by individuals; and education is the one thing in which the individual has direct and despotic power.

(ILN, "Education and Ethics," 1-15-10)

Education is only truth in a state of transmission; and how can we pass on truth if it has never come into our hand?

(WWW, IV-5)

But the important point here is only that you cannot anyhow get rid of authority in education; it is not so much (as poor Conservatives say) that parental authority ought to be preserved, as that it cannot be destroyed.

That is the one eternal education; to be sure enough that something is true that you dare to tell it to a child.

The trouble in too many of our modern schools is that the State, being controlled so specially by the few, allows cranks and experiments to go straight to the schoolroom when they have never passed through the Parliament, the public house, the private house, the church, or the marketplace.

Obviously, it ought to be the oldest things that are taught to the youngest people; the assured and experienced truths that are put first to the baby.

But in a school to-day the baby has to submit to a system that is younger than himself.

The flopping infant of four actually has more experience, and has weathered the world longer, than the dogma to which he is made to submit.

Many a school boasts of having the last ideas in education, when it has not even the first idea; for the first idea is that even innocence, divine as it is, may learn something from experience.

In modern practice the free educationists forbid far more things than the old-fashioned educationists.

(WWW, IV-6)

There is one thing at least of which there is never so much as a whisper inside the popular schools; and that is the opinion of the people

The only persons who seem to have nothing to do with the education of the children are the parents.

Modern education means handing down the customs of the minority, and rooting out the customs of the majority.

(WWW, IV-13)

Modern education is founded on the principle that a parent is more likely to be cruel than anybody else.

(SD, ch. 5)

It is impossible to argue at once that the schoolmaster ought to teach everything, and to argue that he will teach nothing that will not please everybody.

It is obviously most unjust that the old believer should be forbidden to teach his old beliefs, while the new believer is free to teach his new beliefs.

It is obviously unfair and unreasonable that secular education should forbid one man to say a religion is true and allow another man to say it is untrue.

It is obviously essential to justice that unsectarian education should cut both ways; and that if the orthodox must cut out the statement that man has a Divine origin, the materialist must cut out the statement that he has a wholly and exclusively bestial origin.

(ILN, "Compulsory Education and the Monkey
Trial," 8-8-25)

People in the past would have been astounded to be told that children could not stay in their own homes to help their own parents, but were driven by the policeman to go to a particular kind of school.

(ILN, "The Presumption of Progress," 12-19-25)

The ordinary man had a right to judge of his children's health, and generally to bring up children to the best of his ability; that is the objection to many interpretations of modern State education.

(OS, ch. 6)

A great many of us think that education, in its modern compulsory form, has got very much into a rut and is likely to become as narrow as any other routine.

(ILN, "Bowing Down to the New Religion," 4-13-29)

He regards School, not as a normal social institution to be fitted into other social institutions, like Home and Church and State, but as some sort of entirely super-normal and miraculous moral factory in which perfect men and women are made by magic.

To this idolatry of School he is ready to sacrifice Home and History and Humanity, with all its instincts and possibilities, at a moment's notice.

To this idol he will make any sacrifice; especially human sacrifice.

But I dislike it, not because I dislike education, but because, given the modern philosophy, education is turned against itself, destroying that very sense of variety and proportion which it is the object of education to give.

No man who worships education has got the best out of education; no man who sacrifices everything to education is even educated.

The moment men begin to care more for education than for religion, they begin to care more for ambition than for education.

There begins to be a mere vanity in being educated; whether it be self-educated or merely State-educated.

(ILN, "The Worship of Education," 4-26-08)

But if I say that one workman is capable of deciding about the education of one child, that he has the right to select a certain school or resist a certain system, I shall have all those progressive papers roaring at me as a rotten reactionary.

(ILN, "Living For the Future," 5-31-30)

No period before our own ever dreamed of the sort of universal persecution that is called Compulsory Education.

(ILN, "Einstein on War," 5-16-31)

But there is something to be said for the idea of teaching everything to somebody, as compared with the modern notion of teaching nothing, and the same sort of nothing, to everybody.

(ILN, "Theorising About Human Society," 10-3-31)

But I am not now arguing which philosophy is the better; I am only pointing out that every education teaches a philosophy; if not by dogma then by suggestion, by implication, by atmosphere.

If it does not all combine to convey some general view of life, it is not education at all.
(CM, "The New Case For Catholic Schools")

[see also: Agnosticism, Dogmatism, Home Schooling, Modernism, Secularism, Skepticism, Tolerance]

Efficiency

But, as far as I can make out, "efficiency" means that we ought to discover everything about a machine except what it is for.

That is, it is futile because it only deals with actions after they have been performed.

It has no philosophy for incidents before they happen; therefore it has no power of choice.
(WWW, I-2)

Ego

Now, the psychological discovery is merely this, that whereas it had been supposed that the fullest possible enjoyment is to be found by extending our ego to infinity, the truth is that the fullest possible enjoyment is to be found by reducing our ego to zero.
(H, ch. 12)

Empires

Thoroughly diseased institutions are always praised as being in a state of brutal and invincible health – like empires.
> (ILN, "The Survival of Christmas," 1-11-08)

The British Empire may annex what it likes, it will never annex England.
> (TRE, ch. 26)

It is commonplace that empires pass away, because empires were never very important.

Empires are frivolous things, the fringes of a sprawling culture that has sprawled too far.
> (ILN, "The Spirit of Europe," 1-11-30)

Men believed in the British Empire precisely because they had nothing else to believe in.
> (A, ch. 6)

[see also: Crusades, "Dark Ages," Greeks, History, History (Church), Hypocrisy (of Christians), Inquisition, Middle Ages, Renaissance, Tolerance, Victorianism, War, War (and Christianity)]

Environment

It is a troublesome thing, environment, for it sometimes works positively and sometimes negatively, and more often between the two.

A beautiful environment may make a child love beauty; it may make him bored with beauty; most likely the two effects will mix and neutralise each other.

Most likely, that is, the environment will make hardly any difference at all.

As it is therefore quite doubtful whether a person will go specially with his environment or specially against his environment, I cannot comfort myself with the thought that the modern discussions about environment are of much practical value.

(TRE, ch. 18)

It may be that the Highlanders are poetical because they inhabit mountains; but are the Swiss prosaic because they inhabit mountains?

It may be the Swiss have fought for freedom because they had hills; did the Dutch fight for freedom because they hadn't?

Environment might work negatively as well as positively.

The Swiss may be sensible, not in spite of their wild skyline, but because of their wild skyline.

The Flemings may be fantastic artists, not in spite of their dull skyline, but because of it.

(WWW, IV-3)

[see also: Anthropology, Ceremony, Compartmentalization, Customs, Man, Man (Smallness of), Nationality, Sociology]

Environmentalism; Conservationism

But we have lived to see a sect that does not look down at the insects, but looks up at the insects, that asks us essentially to bow down and worship beetles, like ancient Egyptians.

(WWW, V-1)

All sane men have assumed that, while a man may be right to feel benevolently towards the jungle, he is also right to treat it as something that may be put to use, and something which he may refuse to assist indefinitely for its own sake at his own expense.

(ILN, "About Means and Ends," 12-11-26)

[see also: Abortion, Animal Rights, Man, Morality, Nature, Vegetarianism]

Eugenics

Eugenics is not merely a sham science, it is a dead science; a great deal more dead than astrology.

(ILN, "Socialistic Morality," 3-26-10)

They have no Science of Eugenics at all, but they do really mean that if we will give ourselves up to be vivisected they may very probably have one some day.

(EUG, I-8)

There is one strong, startling, outstanding thing about Eugenics, and that is its meanness.

(EUG, II-5)

It is a principle whereby the deepest things of flesh and spirit must have the most direct relation with the dictatorship of the State.

(EUG, II-6)

[see also: Abortion, Abstinence, Birth Control, Contraception, Euphemisms, Euthanasia, Feminism, Sexuality]

Euphemisms and Pseudonyms   ·

We have grown used to a habit of calling things by the wrong names and supporting them by the wrong arguments; and even doing the right thing for the wrong cause.

It is a parliament of Alice in Wonderland, where the name of a thing is different from what it is called, and even from what its name is called.

(NJ, ch. 7)

Everything is to be recommended to the public by some sort of synonym which is really a pseudonym.

They introduce their heresies under new and carefully complementary names; as the Furies were called the Eumenides.

When someone wishes to wage a social war against what all normal people have regarded as a social decency, the very first thing he does is find some artificial term that shall sound relatively decent.

He has no more of the real courage that would pit vice against virtue than the ordinary advertiser has the courage to advertise ale as arsenic.

With the passions which are natural to youth we all sympathise; with the pain that often arises from loyalty and duty we all sympathise still more; but nobody need sympathise with publicity experts picking pleasant expressions for unpleasant things; and I for one prefer the coarse language of our fathers.

(ILN, "The Friends of Frankness, and Euphemism,"
6-30-28)

[see also: Abortion, Eugenics, Euthanasia, Jargon, Language, Newspapers, Novels, Writers]

Euthanasia

Say to them "The persuasive and even coercive powers of the citizen should enable him to make sure that the burden of longevity in the previous generations does not become disproportionate and intolerable, especially to the females?"; say this to them and they sway slightly to and fro like babies sent to sleep in cradles.

Say to them "Murder your mother," and they sit up quite suddenly.

(EUG, I-2)

In the matter of fundamental human rights, nothing can be above Man, except God.

(EUG, I-5)

As for the social justification of murder, that has already begun; and earnest thinkers had better begin at once to think about a nice, inoffensive name for it.

We may call it Life-Control or Free Death, or anything else that has as little to do with the point of it as Companionate Marriage has to do with either marriage or companionship.

(ILN, "The Friends of Frankness, and Euphemism," 6-30-28)

There will be Diocletian persecutions, there will be Dominican crusades, there will be rending of all religious peace and compromise, or even the end of civilization and the world, before the Catholic Church will admit that one single moron, or one single man, "is not worth saving."

(TT, ch. 3)

While we are kicking our grandfather downstairs, we must take care to be very polite to our great-great grandson, who is not yet present; and if a more enlightened ethic should ever justify us in painlessly poisoning our mother, it will be well to distract the attention by dreaming of some perfect Woman of the future who may never need to be poisoned.

(ILN, "Living For the Future," 5-31-30)

[see also: Abortion, Birth Control, Contraception, Eugenics, Euphemisms, Family]

Evil

The difficulty does not arise so much from the mere fact that good and evil are mingled in roughly equal proportions; it arises chiefly from the fact that men always differ about what parts are good and what evil.

(H, ch. 6)

The strongest saints and the strongest sceptics alike took positive evil as the starting-point of their argument.

(O, ch. 2)

[see also: Angels, Cross, Death, Ghosts, Incarnation, Jesus, Mary, Mass, Miracles, Original Sin, Resurrection, Sacramentalism, Saints, Satan & Demons, Sin, Transubstantiation, Trinitarianism]

Experts

Now, one of these four or five paradoxes which should be taught to every infant prattling at his mother's knee is the following: That the more a man looks at a thing, the less he can see it, and the more a man learns a thing the less he knows it.

The Fabian argument of the expert, that the man who is trained should be the man who is trusted would be absolutely unanswerable if it were really true that a man who studied a thing and practiced it every day went on seeing more and more of its significance.

(TRE, ch. 11)

[see also: Common Sense, Critics, Gentlemen, "Higher Culture," Humanitarianism, Intelligentsia, Man (Common), Prigs]

Fairy Tales

The fairy-tale means extraordinary things as seen by ordinary people.

> (ILN, "Education By Fairy Tales," 12-2-05)

We all believe fairy-tales, and live in them.

> (H, ch. 20)

Fairy tales mean the uncommon things as seen by the common people.

> (CD, ch. 4)

If you really read fairy-tales, you will observe that one idea runs from one end of them to the other – the idea that peace and happiness can only exist on some condition.

> (ILN, "The Ethics of Fairy-Tales," 2-29-08)

The fairy tale discusses what a sane man will do in a mad world.

(O, ch. 2)

Fairyland is nothing but the sunny country of common sense.

Thus I have said that stories of magic alone can express my sense that life is not only a pleasure but a kind of eccentric privilege.

(O, ch. 4)

It is far easier to believe in a million fairy tales than to believe in one man who does not like fairy tales.

In the fairy tales the cosmos goes mad; but the hero does not go mad.

(TRE, ch. 16)

Fairy tales, then, are not responsible for producing in children fear, or any of the shapes of fear; fairy tales do not give the child the idea of the evil or the ugly; that is in the child already, because it is in the world already.

The baby has known the dragon intimately ever since he had an imagination.

What the fairy tale provides for him is a St. George to kill the dragon.

Exactly what the fairy tale does is this: it accustoms him for a series of clear pictures to the idea that these

limitless terrors had a limit, that these shapeless enemies have enemies in the knights of God, that there is
something in the universe more mystical than darkness,
and stronger than strong fear.

(TRE, ch. 17)

That sane half scepticism which was found in all
rustics, in all ghost tales and fairy tales, seems to be a
lost secret.

(AD, ch. 15)

The fairy-tale, on the other hand, absolutely revolves
on the pivot of human personality.

(SL, "Aesop's Fables" [1912])

There is no better test of the truth of serious fiction
than the simple truths to be found in a fairy tale or an
old ballad.

(FVF, ch. 12)

Peter Pan does not belong to the world of Pan but
the world of Peter.

(EM, II-3)

It is true that I believe in fairy-tales—in the sense
that I marvel so much at what does exist that I am the
readier to admit what might.

(OS, ch. 1)

[see also: Adventure, Children, Chivalry, Imagination, Middle ages, Mythology, Poetry, Romanticism, Stories, Wonder]

Faith

And faith means believing the incredible, or it is no
virtue at all.

But faith is unfashionable, and it is customary on
every side to cast against it the fact that it is a paradox.

Whatever may be the meaning of faith, it must always
mean a certainty about something we cannot prove.

(H, ch. 12)

In other words, we come to the unfathomable idea
of grace and the gift of faith; and I have not the smallest
intention of attempting to fathom it.

It is a theological question of the utmost complexity;
and it is one thing to feel it as a fact and another to define
it as a truth.

But of all these things, that come nearest to the actual
transition of the gift of faith, it is far harder to write than of
the rationalistic and historical preliminaries of the enquiry.

(CCC, ch. 3)

[see also: Asceticism, Confession, Faith (and Reason),
Hope, Incense, Martyrdom, Mysticism, Relics, Robes,
Sabbath, Temptation]

Faith (and Reason)

Thus, for instance, we believe by faith in the existence of other people.

(H, ch. 12)

Some hold the undemonstrable dogma of the existence of God; some the equally undemonstrable dogma of
the existence of the man next door.

(H, ch. 20)

The most orthodox doctors have always maintained
that faith is something superior to reason but not contrary to it.

(ILN, "Education and Ethics," 1-15-10)

Like most people with a taste for Catholic tradition,
I am too much of a rationalist for that; for Catholics are
almost the only people now defending reason.

But I am not talking of the true relations of reason
and mystery, but of the historical fact that mystery has
invaded the peculiar realms of reason; especially the
European realms of the motor and the telephone.

(NJ, ch. 9)

Now what we have really got to hammer into the
heads of all these people, somehow, is that a thinking
man can think himself deeper and deeper into Catholicism, and not deeper and deeper into difficulties about
Catholicism.

We have got to make them see that conversion is
the beginning of an active, fruitful, progressive and even
adventurous life of the intellect.

We have got to explain somehow that the great mysteries like the Blessed Trinity or the Blessed Sacrament
are the starting-points for trains of thought far more

stimulating, subtle and even individual, compared with which all that sceptical scratching is as thin, shallow and dusty as a nasty piece of scandalmongering in a New England village.

(TT, ch. 29)

St. Thomas did not reconcile Christ to Aristotle; he reconciled Aristotle to Christ.

(STA, ch. 1)

The truth is that the historical Catholic Church began by being Platonist; by being rather too Platonist.

The Christian Fathers were much more like the Neo-Platonists than were the scholars of the Renaissance; who were only Neo-Neo-Platonists.

(STA, ch. 3)

[see also: Apologetics, Argument, Ideas, Idealism, Paradox (in Christianity), Philosophy, Reason & Logic, Science (and Religion), Theism, Truth]

Family, The

The modern writers who have suggested, in a more or less open manner, that the family is a bad institution, have generally confined themselves to suggesting, with much sharpness, bitterness, or pathos, that perhaps the family is not always very congenial.

Of course the family is a good institution because it is uncongenial.

It is, as the sentimentalists say, like a little kingdom, and, like most other little kingdoms, is generally in a state of something resembling anarchy.

It is exactly because our brother George is not interested in our religious difficulties, but is interested in the Trocadero Restaurant, that the family has some of the bracing qualities of the commonwealth.

The men and women who, for good reasons and bad, revolt against the family, are, for good reasons and bad, simply revolting against mankind.

It is romantic because it is arbitrary.

When we step into the family, by the act of being born, we do step into a world which is incalculable, into a world which has its own strange laws, into a world which could do without us, into a world that we have not made.

In other words, when we step into the family we step into a fairy-tale.

Of all these great limitations and frameworks which fashion and create the poetry and variety of life, the family is the most definite and important.

Hence it is misunderstood by the moderns, who imagine that romance would exist most perfectly in a complete state of what they call liberty.

(H, ch. 14)

It can, perhaps, be most correctly stated by saying that, even if the man is the head of the house, he knows he is the figurehead.

(ATC, ch. 2)

Without the family we are helpless before the State, which in our modern case is the Servile State.

To use a military metaphor, the family is the only formation in which the charge of the rich can be repulsed.

(SD, ch. 2)

But if it be true that Socialism attacks the family in theory, it is far more certain that Capitalism attacks it in practice.

In the last resort, the only people who either can or will give individual care, to each of the individual children, are their individual parents.

(SD, ch. 5)

A man saying that he will treat other people's children as his own is exactly like a man saying that he will treat other people's wives as his own.

The notion of making the head of a humble family really independent and responsible, like a citizen, has really vanished from the mind of most of the realists of our real world.

(AIS, ch. 1)

But, so far as we are concerned, what has broken up households and encouraged divorces, and treated the old domestic virtues with more and more open contempt, is the epoch and Power of Capitalism.

It is Capitalism that has forced a moral feud and a commercial competition between the sexes; that has destroyed the influence of the parent in favour of the influence of the employer; that has driven men from their homes to look for jobs; that has forced them to live near their factories or their firms instead of near their families; and, above all, that has encouraged, for commercial reasons, a parade of publicity and garish novelty, which is in its nature the death of all that was called dignity and modesty by our mothers and fathers.

(WEL, "Three Foes of the Family")

If individuals have any hope of protecting their freedom, they must protect their family life.

(WEL, "St. Thomas More")

[see also: Divorce, Eugenics, Feminism, Fidelity, Gender Differences, Home, Marriage, Motherhood, Mothers-in-Law, Sexuality, Wives]

Fanatics

To know the best theories of existence and to choose the best from them (that is, to the best of our own strong conviction) appears to us the proper way to be neither bigot nor fanatic, but something more firm than a bigot and more terrible than a fanatic, a man with a definite opinion.

(H, ch. 20)

[see also: Conspiratorialism, Despair, Madness, Moods, Optimism, Pessimism, Resignation, Suicide]

Fashions and Fads

There is no intrinsic and eternal significance about any fashion; none about a lost fashion; none whatever about the latest fashion.

(ILN, "The Younger Pagans," 8-21-26)

Anything that is fashionable is on the brink of being old-fashioned.

(ILN, "Keeping Old Words New," 8-28-26)

But I do find it amusing to watch the continual rise of new fashions, which is invariably the return of old fashions.

(ILN, "Disputes About Artistic Tastes," 12-17-27)

Nearly all the talk about what is advanced and what is antiquated has become a sort of giggling excitement about fashions.

(TT, ch. 6)

And the moral of it is that nothing grows old so quickly as what is new.

Each generation of rebels in turn is remembered by the next, not as the pioneers who began the march, or started to break away from the old conventions; but as the old convention from which only the very latest rebels have dared to break away.

(AIS, ch. 32)

Men who lose traditions abandon themselves to conventions; but the conventions are more fleeting than fashions.

(CM, "The Romance of a Rascal")

[see also: Conformity, Nonconformity (Christian), Spirit of the Age (*Zeitgeist*)]

Feminism; Unisexism

Thus, for instance, people talk with a quite astonishing gravity about the inequality or equality of the sexes; as if there could possibly be any inequality between a lock and a key.

A woman is only inferior to man in the matter of being not so manly; she is inferior in nothing else.

If everything is trying to be green, some things will be greener than others; but there is an immortal and indestructible equality between green and red.

(CD, ch. 10)

It is plain on the face of it, whatever else is doubtful, that human society does permit, and must permit, some noble functions to be confined to one sex.

If there be any unjust sex-privilege, surely this is one, that in the cradle and the nursery one sex is put at a disadvantage.

We let loose hardy and matured females upon helpless and innocent males.

But if the special privilege of woman is a mistake, then the whole human race is a mistake.

(ILN, "Female Suffrage and the New Theology,"
3-16-07)

If a man tried to regard a woman as a chattel his life would not be worth living for twenty-four hours.

But that any living man ever felt like that, that any living man ever felt as if a woman was a piece of furniture, with which one could do what he liked, is starkly incredible.

(ILN, "How and Why Women Vote," 4-6-07)

Just as an eastern newspaper is a victory of Western methods, so the Feminist movement is a surrender to the masculine intelligence.

(ILN, "American Slaves and Female Emancipation,"
8-1-08)

Ever since we have any human records, women have done almost nothing else but criticise the weaknesses of men.

(ILN, "Listening to Modernist Arguments," 8-29-08)

We knew quite well that nothing is necessary to the country except that the men should be men and the women women.

Suddenly, without warning, the women have begun to say all the nonsense that we ourselves hardly believed when we said it.

(WWW, III-7)

I am not satisfied with the statement that my
daughter must have unwomanly powers because she has
unwomanly wrongs.

(WWW, III-12)

It is utterly astounding to note the way in which
modern writers and talkers miss this plain, wide, and
overwhelming fact: one would suppose woman a victim
and nothing else.

The sexes cannot wish to abolish each other; and if
we allow them any sort of permanent opposition it will
sink into something as base as a party system.

(MM, ch. 1)

And it is the convention of journalism at this moment
to support what is feminist against what is feminine.

(FVF, ch. 27)

As a matter of psychology, it would be foolish to
insult even an unfeminine feminist in order to awaken a
delicate chivalry towards females.

(OS, ch. 6)

There is the obvious contradiction that feminism
often means the refusal to be feminine.

(ILN, "The Narrowness of the New Art," 8-18-28)

[see also: Abortion, Abstinence, Birth Control, Chiv-
alry, Contraception, Divorce, Eugenics, Euphemisms,
Euthanasia, Family, Fidelity, Gender Differences, Home,
Marriage, Sexuality, Wives]

Fiction

And the same civilization, the chivalric European civilization which asserted freewill in the thirteenth century, produced the thing called "fiction" in the eighteenth.

(H, ch. 14)

Fiction means the common things as seen by the uncommon people.

As our world advances through history towards its present epoch, it becomes more specialist, less democratic, and folklore turns gradually into fiction.

(CD, ch. 4)

Journalism only tells us what men are doing; it is fiction that tells us what they are thinking, and still more what they are feeling.

(ILN, "The Independence of Women," 4-21-23)

In short, the old literature, both great and trivial, was built on the idea that there is a purpose in life, even if it is not always completed in this life; and it really was interesting to follow the stages of such a purpose; from the meeting to the wedding, from the wedding to the bells, and from the bells to the church.

(ILN, "The Sloppiness of the Modern Novel – and Modern Thought," 3-8-30)

[see also: Art and Artists, Language, Jargon, Newspapers, Novels, Poetry, Stories, Writers]

Fidelity

They appear to imagine that the ideal of constancy was a yoke mysteriously imposed on mankind by the devil, instead of being, as it is, a yoke consistently imposed by all lovers on themselves.

It is the nature of love to bind itself, and the institution of marriage merely paid the average man the compliment of taking him at his word.

(DEF, ch. 2)

If I vow to be faithful I must be cursed when I am unfaithful, or there is no fun in vowing.

(O, ch. 7)

It is quite true that the lovers feel their love eternal, and independent of oaths; but it is emphatically not true that they do not desire to take the oath.

The time when they want the vow is exactly the time when they do not need it.

(ILN, "The Bonds of Love," 7-2-10)

The vow is a voluntary loyalty; and the marriage vow is marked among ordinary oaths of allegiance by the fact that the allegiance is also a choice.

(SD, ch. 2)

To whom should a man keep his word, if not to his wife?

(ILN, "Modern Stories and Modern Morality," 7-3-26)

[see also: Divorce, Family, Home, Marriage, Sexuality, Wives]

Fools; "Characters"

Which of us has not known, for instance, a great rustic?—a character so incurably characteristic that he seemed to break through all canons about cleverness or stupidity; we do not know whether he is an enormous idiot or an enormous philosopher; we know only that he is enormous, like a hill.

These great, grotesque characters are almost entirely to be found where Dickens found them—among the poorer classes.

It is in private life that we find the great characters.

The great fool is he in whom we cannot tell which is the conscious and which the unconscious humour; we laugh with him and laugh at him at the same time.

(CD, ch. 10)

There is a certain solid use in fools.

It is not so much that they rush in where angels fear to tread, but rather that they let out what devils intend to do.

Some perversion of folly will float about nameless and pervade a whole society; then some lunatic gives it a name, and henceforth it is harmless.

(AD, ch. 16)

[see also: Hilarity, Humor, Satire, Wit]

Friendship; Camaraderie

For friendship implies individuality; whereas comradeship really implies the temporary subordination, if not the temporary swamping of individuality.

Friends are the better for being two; but comrades are the better for being two million.

Friendship becomes comradeship when you have forgotten the presence of your friend.

You are addressing the abstract thing, the club, which, when two or three are gathered together (of the male sort at least) is always in the midst of them.

To forget a male friend is only to behave like a comrade.

But to forget a woman friend is only to behave like a cad.

She is herself; he is the club.
                    (AWD, "A Case of Comrades" [1908])

Comradeship is at the most only one half of human life; the other half is Love, a thing so different that one might fancy it had been made for another universe.

But very broadly speaking it may still be said that women stand for the dignity of love and men for the dignity of comradeship.

The affections in which women excel have so much more authority and intensity that pure comradeship would be washed away if it were not rallied and guarded in clubs, corps, colleges, banquets and regiments.

No one has even begun to understand comradeship who does not accept with it a certain hearty eagerness in eating, drinking, or smoking, an uproarious materialism which to many women appears only hoggish.

Anyone who has known true comradeship in a club or in a regiment, knows that it is impersonal.

(WWW, II-2)

Business will have nothing to do with leisure; business will have no truck with comradeship; business will pretend to no patience with all the legal fictions and fantastic handicaps by which comradeship protects its egalitarian ideal.

(WWW, II-4)

[see also: Cliques, Conversation, Neighbors, Silent Types, Singing, Talkers]

Gender Differences

The reason why men have from the beginning of literature talked about women as if they were more or less mad, is simply because women are natural, and men, with their formalities and social theories, are very artificial.

(SL, "The Philosophy of Islands" [1903])

Men are much more sentimental than women; women are rather cynical than otherwise.

Generally speaking, it would be much easier for a pretty woman to bamboozle an ordinary sensible man than for a merely handsome man to bamboozle an ordinary sensible woman.

(ILN, "How and Why Women Vote," 4-6-07)

For the two things that a healthy person hates most between heaven and hell are a woman who is not dignified and a man who is.

(ATC, ch. 2)

There are no such things as women.

There is only the woman you are at this particular moment afraid of or in love with, or inclined to reverence or inclined to assassinate.

(AWD, "A Case of Comrades" [1908])

Women are all anarchists just as saints are all anarchists.

That is, they do not see the need of rules when they are dealing with realities.

(ILN, "Female Suffrage and Responsibility," 2-27-09)

For a man and a woman, as such, are incompatible.

(WWW, I-7)

Women speak to each other; men speak to the subject they are speaking about.

Many an honest man has sat in a ring of his five best friends under heaven and forgotten who was in the room while he explained some system.

This is not peculiar to intellectual men; men are all theoretical, whether they are talking about God or about golf.

Men are all impersonal; that is to say, republican.

No one remembers after a really good talk who has said the good things.

Every man speaks to a visionary multitude; a mystical cloud, that is called the club.

(WWW, II-2)

A circle of small pedants sit on an upper platform, and pass unanimously (in a meeting of none) that there is no difference between the social duties of men and of women, the social instruction of men or of children.

(AWD, "What is Right With the World" [1910])

And this matter of the functions of the sexes is primarily a matter of the instincts; sex and breathing are about the only two things that generally work best when they are least worried about.

(MM, ch. 1)

The sexes can work together in a school-room just as they can breakfast together in a breakfast-room; but neither makes any difference to the fact that the boys go off to a boyish companionship which the girls would think disgusting, while the girls go off to a girl companionship which the boys would think literally insane.

(CM, "Two Stubborn Pieces of Iron")

[see also: Chivalry, Family, Feminism, Fidelity, Friendship, Home, Marriage, Motherhood, Sexuality, Wives]

Gentlemen

The modern gentleman is not the man who knows how to be polite; he is the man who knows how to be rude in an entirely gentlemanly manner.

(AWD, "On Manners" [1902])

The gentleman is a Stoic because he is a sort of savage, because he is filled with a great elemental fear that some stranger will speak to him.

That is why a third-class carriage is a community, while a first-class carriage is a place of wild hermits.

(H, ch. 15)

Gentlemen do tend to be, as Matthew Arnold said, barbarians.

(ILN, "The Millionaires' Freak Dinner," 3-24-06)

Refinement is not virtue; silence is not virtue (it is almost always vice); being a gentleman is not being a good man, but quite often the reverse.

(ILN, "Undergraduate Ragging," 12-28-07)

But in Christian society we have always thought the gentleman a sort of joke, though I admit that in some great crusades and councils he earned the right to be called a practical joke.

(O, ch. 7)

Thus there is the man who wishes first to prove that he is a gentleman, and only proves two things: first, that he is vulgar enough to prefer being a gentleman to being a man; and second, that he has a hideously stunted and half-witted notion even of being a gentleman.

(ILN, "A Definition of Vulgarity," 6-8-29)

[see also: Common Sense, Critics, Experts, "Higher Culture," Humanitarianism, Intelligentsia, Man (Common), Prigs]

Ghosts

If you ask me why ghosts and devils are denied, while bats and shooting stars are reluctantly conceded, I can only answer that it is the not interesting and by no means undignified thing which we have to call Bigotry.

(ILN, "Objections to Spiritualism," 10-30-09)

 I do not see ghosts; I only see their inherent probability.

(TRE, ch. 4)

A man who will not listen to any evidence in favour of ghosts or witches may (especially in his own opinion) possess sense; but what exactly he does not possess is common-sense.

(ILN, "Spiritualism and Agnosticism," 1-12-29)

But to answer a ghost by saying, "This is the twentieth century," is in itself quite unmeaning; like seeing somebody commit a murder and then saying, "But this is the second Tuesday in August!"

(TT, ch. 15)

[see also: Angels, Cross, Death, Evil, Incarnation, Jesus, Mary, Mass, Miracles, Original Sin, Resurrection, Sacramentalism, Saints, Satan & Demons, Sin, Spiritualism, Transubstantiation, Trinitarianism]

Gnosticism

Now, being purely spiritual is opposed to the very essence of religion.

All religions, high and low, true and false, have always had one enemy, which is the purely spiritual.
(ILN, "Faith Healing and Medicine," 11-5-10)

The creed declared that man was sinful, but it did not declare that life was evil, and it proved it by damning those who did.

(EM, II-4)

[see also: Heresies, Orthodoxy, Paganism, Reincarnation, Religion (Comparative), Spiritualism, Superstition]

Government

Men govern by debate, not because debate is necessary to government, but because debate is necessary to men.
(ILN, "Women, Camaraderie, and Politics," 5-26-06)

If our faith comments on government at all, its comment must be this—that the man should rule who does *not* think that he can rule.

(O, ch. 7)

Men have never wearied of political justice; they have wearied of waiting for it.

(WWW, I-6)

The English Parliament actually cares for everything except veracity.

(WWW, IV-11)

For at present we all tend to one mistake; we tend to make politics too important.
(AWD, "What is Right With the World" [1910])

We are ruled by ignorant people.
(UTO, "The Empire of the Ignorant")

We have party governments which consist of people who pretend to agree when they really disagree.

We have party debates which consist of people who pretend to disagree when they really agree.

We have whole parties named after things they no longer support, or things they would never dream of proposing.
(NJ, ch. 7)

Government has become ungovernable; that is, it cannot leave off governing.

The chief feature of our time is the meekness of the mob and the madness of the government.
(EUG, I-8)

[see also: Anarchy, Aristocracy, Caesaropapism, Conservatism, Democracy, Law, Liberalism (Political), Monarchy, Nationalism, Nazism, Patriotism, Politicians, Revolution, Socialism, Spain (Civil War), Tolerance, Voting]

Greeks, Ancient

If future ages happened to record nothing else about Socrates except that he owned his title to be the wisest of men because he knew that he knew nothing, they would be able to deduce from that the height and energy of his civilisation, the glory that was Greece.

(VT, ch. 15)

The vast Greek philosophy could fit easier into the small city of Athens than into the immense Empire of Persia.

(TRE, ch. 23)

This deep truth of the danger of insolence, or being too big for our boots, runs through all the great Greek tragedies and makes them great.

(EM, I-5)

For the Greeks were the obvious leaders of the march of mankind, and especially of the Mediterranean civilization; and to some extent it is true that what went wrong with them was their moral self-control and self-respect; so that the lordship of light and order, and the making of modern Europe, passed to the little Latin village on the Tiber.

But perhaps the greatest of Greek tragedies was the tragedy of the Greeks.

(ILN, "Dr. Freud and Ancient Myth," 10-26-29)

[see also: Argument, Crusades, "Dark Ages," Empires, History, History (Church), Ideas, Inquisition, Middle Ages, Philosophy, Reason & Logic, Renaissance, Tolerance, Victorianism, War, War (and Christianity)]

Guilds (Mediaeval)

We say the Guilds were good without in the least suggesting that they were perfect; they accuse us of saying they were perfect when we have managed to prove that they were good.

It is not a fancy but a fact that the mediaeval world tried to establish a Just Price, where the modern world is at the mercy of a merciless anarchy in prices.

It is not a fancy but a fact that the old Guilds, unlike the modern Trade Unions, could prevent the inequality of Capitalism without being tempted to the fad of Communism.
(ILN, "More Myths, Mediaeval and Victorian," 6-2-23)

The case for the Guild has nothing to do with the romance of mediaevalism; nothing whatever.

Now the Guild method is no more mediaeval than it is modern, in so far as it is a principle apart from time.
(ILN, "The Guild Idea," 1-5-29)

[see also: Capitalism, Distributism, Middle Ages, Philanthropy, Poor, Publicity, Simplicity, Socialism, Thrift, Wealth]

$\mathcal{H}$

Happiness and Joy

Christianity is itself so jolly a thing that it fills the possessor of it with a certain silly exuberance, which sad and high-minded Rationalists might reasonably mistake for mere buffoonery and blasphemy; just as their prototypes, the sad and high-minded Stoics of old Rome, did mistake the Christian joyousness for buffoonery and blasphemy.

Happiness is a mystery like religion, and should never be rationalized.

For any kind of pleasure a totally different spirit is required; a certain shyness, a certain indeterminate hope, a certain boyish expectation.

Ultimately a man can enjoy nothing except religion.
(H, ch. 7)

But I am more and more convinced that neither in
your special spices nor in mine, neither in honey-pots nor
quart-pots, neither in mustard nor in music, nor in any
other distraction from life, is the secret we are all seeking, the secret of enjoying life.

You have to be happy in those quiet moments when
you remember that you are alive; not in those noisy
moments when you forget.

(SL, "The Spice of Life" [1936])

Religion might approximately be defined as the
power which makes us joyful about the things that
matter.

(CM, "The Frivolous Man")

Hedonism

Everywhere there is the persistent and insane
attempt to obtain pleasure without paying for it.

(DEF, ch. 2)

There is on the earth a race of revellers who do,
under all their exuberance, fundamentally regard time
as an enemy.

(TWE, ch. 7)

For there is but an inch of difference between the
cushioned chamber and the padded cell.

(CD, ch. 6)

In this world we cannot have pure pleasure.

This is partly because pure pleasure would be dangerous to us and to our neighbours.

(TRE, ch. 23)

To the healthy soul there is something in the very nature of certain pleasures which warns us that they are exceptions, and that if they become rules they will become very tyrannical rules.

(AD, ch. 26)

The idea of the gay and thoughtless man of fashion, intoxicated with pagan delights, is a figment invented entirely by religious people who never met any such man in their lives.

(CM, "The Frivolous Man")

[see also: Agnosticism, Atheism, Determinism, Liberalism (Theological), Materialism, Modernism, Pragmatism, Progress (Idea of), Secularism, Skepticism, Utopias]

Heresies

Truths turn into dogmas the instant that they are disputed.

Thus every man who utters a doubt defines a religion.

And the scepticism of our time does not really destroy the beliefs, rather it creates them; gives them their limits and their plain and defiant shape.

We who are Christians never knew the great philosophic common sense which inheres in that mystery until the anti-Christian writers pointed it out to us.

(H, ch. 20)

To have fallen into any of those open traps of error and exaggeration which fashion after fashion and sect after sect set along the historic path of Christendom— that would indeed have been simple.

To have fallen into any one of the fads from Gnosticism to Christian Science would indeed have been obvious and tame.

But to have avoided them all has been one whirling adventure; and in my vision the heavenly chariot flies thundering through the ages, the dull heresies sprawling and prostrate, the wild truth reeling but erect.

(O, ch. 6)

An error is more menacing than a crime, for an error begets crimes.

(TRE, ch. 34)

A hundred mad dogs of heresy have worried man from the beginning; but it was always the dog that died.

(SD, ch. 8)

Every heresy has been an effort to narrow the Church.

(SF, ch. 10)

And it is rather hard that the Catholics should be blamed by the same critics for persecuting the heretics and also for sympathising with the heresy.

(EM, II-4)

In all of them you find that some Catholic dogma is, first, taken for granted; then exaggerated into an error; and then generally reacted against and rejected as an error, bringing the individual in question a few steps back again on the homeward road.

(CCC, ch. 4)

These people merely take the modern mood, with much in it that is amiable and much that is anarchical and much that is merely dull and obvious, and then require any creed to be cut down to fit that mood.

(CCC, ch. 5)

A morbid or unbalanced Catholic takes one idea out of the thousandfold throng of Catholic ideas; and announces that he cares for that Catholic idea more than for Catholicism.

(TT, ch. 32)

A heresy is a truth that hides all the other truths.

(WEL, "St. Thomas More")

The heretic is a man who loves his truth more than truth itself.

(CM, "On Reading")

[see also: Gnosticism, Orthodoxy, Paganism, Reincarnation, Religion (Comparative), Spiritualism, Superstition]

Heroes

All men can be criminals, if tempted; all men can be heroes, if inspired.

(H, ch. 12)

For instance, we all have fancy for an entirely fearless man, a hero; and the Achilles of Homer still remains.

But exactly the thing we do not know about Achilles is how far he was possible.

(CD, ch. 12)

"Higher Criticism" (of the Bible)

The book of Job may have grown gradually just as Westminster Abbey grew gradually.

But the people who made the old folk poetry, like the people who made Westminster Abbey, did not attach that importance to the actual date and the actual author, that importance which is entirely the creation of the almost insane individualism of modern times.

Many people have maintained the characteristic formula of modern skepticism, that Homer was not written by Homer, but by another person of the same name.

(JOB)

And it is stark hypocrisy to pretend that nine-tenths of the higher critics and scientific evolutionists and professors of comparative religion are in the least impartial.

(EM, Introduction)

The date of the Fourth Gospel, which at one time was steadily growing later and later, is now steadily growing earlier and earlier; until critics are staggered at the dawning and dreadful possibility that it might be something like what it professes to be.

(EM, II-4)

For it is a principle of all truly scientific Higher Criticism that any text you do not happen to like is a later monkish interpolation.

(ILN, "The Extension of the Family," 3-5-27)

Quite apart from miracles, I never could quite understand why a Great Sea Serpent should not be big; or even big enough to swallow a moderate-sized Hebrew prophet.

(ILN, "The Bible and the Sceptics," 4-20-29)

They had no more read Luke than they had read Loisy; they merely took it on trust that Loisy had somehow discredited Luke.

(ILN, "'Who Moved the Stone?'," 4-5-30)

[see also: Bible, Prophets, Revelation (Book of), *Sola Scriptura*]

"Higher Culture"

The effect of it on the rich men who are free for it is so horrible that it is worse than any of the other amusements of the millionaire—worse than gambling, worse even than philanthropy.

The higher culture is sad, cheap, impudent, unkind, without honesty and without ease.

(ILN, "Women, Communism, and the Higher Culture," 4-7-06)

The Higher Culture to which I was referring is a quite fleeting and fundamentally caddish sort of culture, filling up the gap which everyone has felt since we gave up real religion and real politics; since we gave up thinking about God and fighting about man.

(ILN, "Women, Worrying, and the Higher Culture," 5-12-06)

[see also: Common Sense, Critics, Experts, Gentlemen, Humanitarianism, Intelligentsia, Man (Common), Prigs]

Hilarity and Merriment

Wherever you have belief you will have hilarity, wherever you have hilarity you will have some dangers.

(H, ch. 6)

No one can be really hilarious but the serious man.

The thing called high spirits is possible only to the spiritual.

(H, ch. 7)

There is nothing to which a man must give himself up with more faith and self-abandonment than to genuine laughter.

(TWE, ch. 6)

[see also: Fools, Humor, Satire, Wit]

History and Historians

But if there really be anything of the nature of progress, it must mean, above all things, the careful study and assumption of the whole of the past.

(H, ch. 12)

To study humanity in the present is like studying a mountain with a magnifying glass; to study it in the past is like studying it through a telescope.

(VT, ch. 14)

Hence the responsibility of those giving truth through popular histories must be specially judged by whether their pictures are really meant to help the history or only to help the sale.

(ILN, "Truth and Lies in Popular Histories," 11-9-07)

History will be wholly false unless it is helped by legend.

I say history will entirely misreport us if we lose tradition.

(ILN, "History and Tradition," 9-12-08)

The highest and noblest thing that history can be is a good story.

It is their affair, not merely to remember that humanity has been wise and great, but to understand the special ways in which it has been weak and foolish.

(ILN, "History and Inspiration," 10-8-10)

Among the many things that leave me doubtful about the modern habit of fixing eyes on the future, none is stronger than this: that all the men in history who have really done anything with the future have had their eyes fixed upon the past.

The originality of Michaelangelo and Shakespeare began with the digging up of old vases and manuscripts.

(WWW, I-4)

History does not consist of completed and crumbling ruins; rather it consists of half-built villas abandoned by a bankrupt-builder.

This world is more like an unfinished suburb than a deserted cemetery.

(WWW, I-5)

History is like some deeply planted tree which, though gigantic in girth, tapers away at last into tiny twigs; and we are in the topmost branches.

(MM, ch. 4)

In the earliest human history, whatever is authentic is universal; and whatever is universal is anonymous.

(SL, "Aesop's Fables" [1912])

And before the historian goes on to show that the heroes of history were lacking in this or that, he will do well to admit that not only heroes, but even historians, are human beings, and may possibly be lacking in something.

As it is, heroes are treated as human beings, but historians are treated as superhuman beings.

(ILN, "The Need For Historical Humility," 8-15-25)

For a man without history is almost in the literal sense half-witted.

(ILN, "Funerals Are For the Living," 12-5-25)

True history should not be divided into periods, but into principles or influences.

(ILN, "Modern Doubts and Questioning," 2-13-26)

But at least history is a joke; and it never fails in that eternal freshness that can surprise us like a practical joke.

(ILN, "The Failure of Prophecies," 4-17-26)

I do not understand why those condemning the past always mention certain facts and not others, and generally in the same form of words.

(ILN, "The Abuses of the Past," 9-17-27)

The simple truth, which some people seem to find it so difficult to understand or to believe, is that what a reasonable man believes in is not this or that *period*, with all its ideas, good or bad, but in certain ideas that may happen to have been present in one period and relatively absent from another period.

(ILN, "The Guild Idea," 1-5-29)

The thing that haunts the historical imagination most, I think, is not Atlantis or Utopia, not the Golden Age or the New Jerusalem, not the Good Old Days or the Good Time Coming, but the gold that men missed or rejected and the good time that might have come.

(ILN, "On Progress in History," 4-27-29)

By a quaint paradox, those who thus assume that history always took the right turning are generally the very people who do not believe there was any special providence to guide it.

(TT, ch. 27)

The difficulty of history is that historians seldom see the simple things, or even the obvious things, because they are too simple and obvious.

(ILN, "The Truth of Mediaeval Times," 1-18-30)

The disadvantage of men not knowing the past is that they do not know the present.

History is a hill or high point of vantage, from which alone men see the town in which they live or the age in which they are living.

(AIS, ch. 21)

But it is obvious that the ordinary modern critic is entirely ignorant of history as a whole.

(AIS, ch. 35)

I only know a very little history; and even that very little is enough to tell me that much more important and powerful and successful persons than myself know no history at all.

(AS, ch. 29)

[see also: Crusades, "Dark Ages," Empires, Greeks, History (Church), Inquisition, Middle Ages, Renaissance, Tolerance, Victorianism, War, War (and Christianity)]

History, Church

The serious opponent of the Latin Church in history, even in the act of showing that it produced great infamies, must know that it produced great saints.

(H, ch. 20)

But the first extraordinary fact which marks this history is this: that Europe has been turned upside down over and over again; and that at the end of each of these revolutions the same religion has again been found on top.

At least five times, therefore, with the Arian and the Albigensian, with the Humanist sceptic, after Voltaire and after Darwin, the Faith has to all appearance gone to the dogs.

(EM, II-6)

[see also: Authority (Religious), Catholicism & Catholics, Catholicity, Christianity, Church (Catholic), Conversion (Catholic), Crusades, "Dark Ages," Development (Doctrinal), Dogma (Catholic), Empires, History, Inquisition, Middle Ages, Orthodoxy, Paganism (and Christianity), Papacy & Popes, Protestantism, Reformation (Catholic), Religion (Organized), Renaissance, Theologians, Tradition]

Home, The; Domesticity

For the average woman is at the head of something with which she can do as she likes; the average man has to obey orders and do nothing else.

(ILN, "Women, Communism, and the Higher Culture," 4-7-06)

Numberless modern women have rebelled against domesticity in theory because they have never known it in practice.

Generally speaking, the cultured class is shrieking to be let out of the decent home, just as the working class is shouting to be let into it.

(WWW, I-6)

But of all the modern notions generated by mere wealth the worst is this: the notion that domesticity is dull and tame.

For the truth is, that to the moderately poor the home is the only place of liberty.

It is the only spot on the earth where a man can alter arrangements suddenly, make an experiment or indulge in a whim.

Everywhere else he goes he must accept the strict rules of the shop, inn, club, or museum that he happens to enter.

(WWW, I-8)

I do not deny that women have been wronged and even tortured; but I doubt if they were ever tortured so much as they are tortured now by the absurd modern attempt to make them domestic empresses and competitive clerks at the same time.

Supposing it to be conceded that humanity has acted at least not unnaturally in dividing itself into two halves, respectively typifying the ideals of special talent and of general sanity (since they are genuinely difficult to combine completely in one mind), it is not difficult to see why the line of cleavage has followed the line of sex, or why the female became the emblem of the universal and the male of the special and superior.

When domesticity, for instance, is called drudgery, all the difficulty arises from a double meaning in the word. If drudgery only means dreadfully hard work, I admit the woman drudges in the home, as a man might drudge at the Cathedral of Amiens or drudge behind a gun at Trafalgar.

But if it means that the hard work is more heavy because it is trifling, colorless and of small import to the soul, then as I say, I give it up; I do not know what the words mean.

(WWW, III-3)

I would give woman, not more rights, but more privileges.

Instead of sending her to seek such freedom as notoriously prevails in banks and factories, I would design specially a house in which she can be free.

(WWW, III-12)

I have never understood what people mean by domesticity being tame; it seems to me one of the wildest of adventures.

(AD, ch. 22)

The place where babies are born, where men die, where the drama of mortal life is acted, is not an office or a shop or a bureau.

(ILN, "Women in the Workplace – and at Home,"
12-18-26)

The narrowness and dullness of domesticity, as described in so many recent plays and novels, was due not to an old tradition but to a new fashion, and a fashion that was rather peculiar to the suburbs of modern industrial cities.

(ILN, "The Extension of the Family," 3-5-27)

Those who believe in the dignity of the domestic tradition, who happen to be the overwhelming majority of mankind, regard the home as a sphere of vast social importance and supreme spiritual significance; and to talk of being confined to it is like talking of being chained to a throne, or set in the seat of judgment as if it were the stocks.

And we cannot assume, as both sides in this curious controversy so often do assume, that bringing forth and rearing and ruling the living beings of the future is a servile task suited to a silly person.

I have never understood myself how this superstition arose: the notion that a woman plays a lowly part in the home and a loftier part outside the home.

(ILN, "The New Woman," 11-16-29)

[see also: Divorce, Family, Feminism, Fidelity, Gender Differences, Marriage, Motherhood, Mothers-in-Law, Sexuality, Wives]

Home-Schooling

This, of course, is connected with the decay of democracy; and is somewhat of a separate subject. Suffice it to say here that when I say that we should instruct our children, I mean that we should do it, not that Mr. Sully or Professor Earl Barnes should do it.

(WWW, IV-6)

Why the workman should be clever enough to vote a curriculum for everybody else's children, but not clever enough to choose one for his own children, I cannot for the life of me imagine.

(ILN, "Living For the Future," 5-31-30)

It is also the age in which the father's right to teach his own children is for the first time denied.

(AIS, ch. 31)

[see also: Education, Family, Home, Motherhood]

Hope

Hope means hoping when things are hopeless, or it is no virtue at all.

For practical purposes it is at the hopeless moment that we require the hopeful man, and the virtue either does not exist at all, or begins to exist at that moment.

Exactly at the instant when hope ceases to be reasonable it begins to be useful.

(H, ch. 12)

Hospitality

Hospitality, the most ancient of human virtues, may appear again in the last days to meet the most modern of social problems, and men may once more remember that Zeus is the protector of the stranger, as they did in the morning of the world.

(ILN, "The Extension of the Family," 3-5-27)

Humanitarianism

There really are some things upon which humanity is practically agreed, but unfortunately these are exactly the things with which the humanitarians do not agree.

But the only men who do not feel this special sanctity of humanity are the humanitarians.

(ILN, "A Uniform Creed For Humanity," 10-3-08)

It is impossible to make a list of the things that humanitarians do not know about humanity.

(ILN, "The Spirit of Europe," 1-11-30)

[see also: Common Sense, Critics, Experts, Gentlemen, "Higher Culture," Intelligentsia, Man (Common), Prigs]

Humility

Whatever may be the reason, we all do warmly respect humility—in other people.

The new philosophy of self-esteem and self-assertion declares that humility is a vice.

It is always the secure who are humble.

(DEF, ch. 12)

It is the humble man who does the big things.

It is the humble man who does the bold things.

(H, ch. 5)

Civilization discovered Christian humility for the same urgent reason that it discovered faith and charity—that is, because Christian civilization had to discover it or die.

To the humble man, and to the humble man alone, the sun is really a sun; to the humble man, and to the humble man alone, the sea is really a sea.

(H, ch. 12)

It is impossible without humility to enjoy anything— even pride.

(O, ch. 3)

The whole difference between a conceited man and a modest one is concerned only with how far he is conscious of those hundred professions in which he would be a failure, of those hundred examinations which he could not pass.

(ILN, "The Ignorance of the People," 2-5-10)

Socrates, the wisest man, knows that he knows nothing.

(EM, II-3)

Humor

But a man cannot indulge in a sham joke, because it is the ruin of a joke to be unintelligible.

(TWE, ch. 4)

But great comedy, the comedy of Shakespeare or Sterne, not only can be, but must be, taken seriously.

(TWE, ch. 6)

Everywhere the robust and uproarious humour has come from the men who were capable not merely of sentimentalism, but a very silly sentimentalism.

For a hearty laugh it is necessary to have touched the heart.

(H, ch. 15)

If there is one thing more than another which any one will admit who has the smallest knowledge of the world, it is that men are always speaking gravely and earnestly and with the utmost possible care about the things that are not important, but always talking frivolously about the things that are.

Funny is the opposite of not funny, and of nothing else.

The question of whether a man expresses himself in a grotesque or laughable phraseology, or in a stately and restrained phraseology, is not a question of motive or of moral state, it is a question of instinctive language and self-expression.

Whether a man chooses to tell the truth in long sentences or short jokes is a problem analogous to whether he chooses to tell the truth in French or German.

But a joke may be exceedingly useful; it may contain the whole earthly sense, not to mention the whole heavenly sense, of a situation.

In the same book in which God's name is fenced from being taken in vain, God himself overwhelms Job with a torrent of terrible levities.

And I should regard any mind which had not got the habit in one form or another of uproarious thinking as being, from the full human point of view, a defective mind.

He ought himself to be importing humour into every controversy; for unless a man is in part a humorist, he is only in part a man.

(H, ch. 16)

And so far as a thing is universal it is full of comic things.

It is the test of a good religion whether you can joke about it.

Whatever is cosmic is comic.

Unless a thing is dignified, it cannot be undignified.

Only man can be absurd: for only man can be dignified.
(ILN, "Spiritualism and Frivolity," 6-9-06)

There seems to be no incompatibility between taking in tragedy and giving out comedy; they are able to run parallel in the same personality.
(CD, ch. 3)

All men can laugh at broad humour, even the subtle humorists.
(CD, ch. 5)

It is so easy to be solemn; it is so hard to be frivolous.
(ATC, ch. 1)

Perspective is really the comic element in everything.
(AD, ch. 27)

The very definition of a joke is that it need have no sense; except that one wild and supernatural sense which we call the sense of humour.

Humour is meant, in a literal sense, to make game of man; that is, to dethrone him from his official dignity and hunt him like game.

It is meant to remind us human beings that we have things about us as ungainly and ludicrous as the nose of the elephant or the neck of the giraffe.

If laughter does not touch a sort of fundamental folly, it does not do its duty in bringing us back to an enormous and original simplicity.

Nothing has been worse than the modern notion that a clever man can make a joke without taking part in it; without sharing in the general absurdity that such a situation creates.

It is unpardonable conceit not to laugh at your own jokes.

Joking is undignified; that is why it is so good for one's soul.

Do not fancy you can be a detached wit and avoid being a buffoon; you cannot.

And every kind of real lark, from acting a charade to making a pun, does consist in restraining one's nine hundred and ninety-nine serious selves and letting the fool loose.

(AD, ch. 31)

But humour always has in it some idea of the humorist himself being at a disadvantage and caught in the entanglements and contradictions of human life.

Nonsense may be described as humour which has for the moment renounced all connection with wit.

It is humour that abandons all attempt at intellectual justification; and does not merely jest at the incongruity of some accident or practical joke, as a by-product of real life, but extracts and enjoys it for its own sake.

(SL, "Humour" [1918])

Every healthy person wishes to make fun of a serious thing; but it is generally almost impossible to make fun of a funny thing.

(CM, "The Pantomime")

[see also: Fools, Hilarity, Satire, Wit]

Hustle and Bustle

One of the great disadvantages of hurry is that it takes such a long time.

(ATC, ch. 1)

Upon this very simple fact of human nature – that bustle always means banality – the whole gigantic modern Press, the palladium of our liberties, is built.

(ILN, "Socialistic Morality," 3-26-10)

[see also: Automobiles, Capitalism, Cities, Communications, Inventions, Traffic]

Hypocrisy (of Christians)

When people impute special vices to the Christian Church, they seem entirely to forget that the world (which is the only other thing there is) has these vices much more.

The Church has been cruel; but the world has been much more cruel.
(ILN, "Francis Thompson and Religious Poetry," 12-14-07)

My point is that the world did not tire of the church's ideal, but of its reality.

Certainly, if the church failed it was largely through the churchmen.

Yet the mediaeval system began to be broken to pieces intellectually, long before it showed the slightest hint of falling to pieces morally.
(WWW, I-5)

The Church is justified, not because her children do not sin, but because they do.
(EM, Introduction)

It is no disgrace to Christianity, it is no disgrace to any great religion, that its counsels of perfection have not made every single person perfect.

If after centuries a disparity is still found between its ideal and its followers, it only means that the religion still maintains the ideal, and the followers still need it.

(ILN, "Buddhism and Christianity," 3-2-29)

The only really fair way of considering the fashionable subject of the crimes of Christendom would be to compare them with the crimes of heathenism; and the normal human practice of the Pagan world.

(TT, ch. 11)

And I feel above all, this simple and forgotten fact; that whether certain charges are or are not true of Catholics, they are quite unquestionably true of everybody else.

The one thing that never seems to cross his mind, when he argues about what the Church is like, is the simple question of what the world would be like without it.

(TT, ch. 13)

[see also: Crusades, Inquisition, Tolerance, War, War (and Christianity)]

Ideas

There is something that does not change; and that is precisely the abstract quality, the invisible idea.

(H, ch. 5)

Ideas are dangerous, but the man to whom they are least dangerous is the man of ideas.

Ideas are dangerous, but the man to whom they are most dangerous is the man of no ideas.

The man of no ideas will find the first idea fly to his head like wine to the head of a teetotaller.

(H, ch. 20)

The man who really thinks he has an idea will always try to explain that idea.

The charlatan who has no idea will always confine himself to explaining that it is much too subtle to be explained.

(MM, ch. 21)

[see also: Apologetics, Argument, Faith (and Reason), Idealism, Paradox (in Christianity), Philosophy, Reason & Logic, Science (and Religion), Theism, Truth]

Idealism and Ideals

Every man is idealistic; only it so often happens that he has the wrong ideal.

People who say that an ideal is a dangerous thing, that it deludes and intoxicates, are perfectly right.

But the ideal which intoxicates most is the least idealistic kind of ideal.

The ideal which intoxicates least is the very ideal ideal; that sobers us suddenly, as all heights and precipices and great distances do.

It is difficult to attain a high ideal; consequently, it is almost impossible to persuade ourselves that we have attained it.

But it is easy to attain a low ideal; consequently, it is easier still to persuade ourselves that we have attained it when we have done nothing of the kind.

(H, ch. 18)

A man's minor actions and arrangements ought to be free, flexible, creative; the things that should be unchangeable are his principles, his ideals.

(TRE, ch. 10)

Idealism is only considering everything in its practical essence.

For the man of action there is nothing but idealism.

This definite ideal is a far more urgent and practical matter in our existing English trouble than any immediate plans or proposals.

(WWW, I-2)

And the upshot of this modern attitude is really this: that men invent new ideals because they dare not attempt old ideals.

(WWW, I-4)

But I have only taken this as the first and most evident case of the general truth: that the great ideals of the past failed not by being outlived (which must mean over-lived), but by not being lived enough.

The Christian ideal has not been tried and found wanting.

It has been found difficult; and left untried.

(WWW, I-5)

There is only one really startling thing to be done with the ideal, and that is to do it.

Christ knew that it would be a more stunning thunderbolt to fulfil the law than to destroy it.

But in the modern world we are primarily confronted with the extraordinary spectacle of people turning to new ideals because they have not tried the old.

Men have not got tired of Christianity; they have never found enough Christianity to get tired of.
(WWW, I-6)

It is a platitude, and none the less true for that, that we need to have an ideal in our minds with which to test all realities.

But it is equally true, and less noted, that we need a reality with which to test ideals.
(AD, ch. 8)

[see also: Apologetics, Argument, Faith (and Reason), Ideas, Paradox (in Christianity), Philosophy, Reason & Logic, Science (and Religion), Theism, Truth]

Imagination

For there cannot be anything less imaginative than mere unreason.

Imagination is a thing of clear images, and the more a thing becomes vague the less imaginative it is.

Similarly, the more a thing becomes wild and lawless the less imaginative it is.
(ILN, "The Millionaires' Freak Dinner," 3-24-06)

For imagination, real imagination, is never a vague thing of vistas.

Real imagination is always materialistic; for imagination consists of images, generally graven images.
(SL, "On Losing One's Head" [1910])

First, I disagree with them when they treat the infantile imagination as a sort of dream; whereas I remember it rather as a man dreaming might remember the world where he was awake.
(ILN, "The Game of Self-Limitation," 2-8-30)

For imagination is almost the opposite of illusion.
(A, ch. 2)

Not verbally, but quite vividly, I knew then, exactly as I know now, that there is something mysterious and perhaps more than mortal about the power and call of imagination.
(CM, "The Pantomime")

[see also: Adventure, Children, Mythology, Poetry, Romanticism, Stories, Wonder]

Incarnation (of Jesus)

I mean that having found the moral atmosphere of the Incarnation to be common sense, I then looked at the established intellectual arguments against the Incarnation and found them to be common nonsense.
(O, ch. 9)

Since that day it has never been quite enough to say that God is in his heaven and all is right with the world, since the rumour that God had left his heavens to set it right.

(EM, II-3)

In the wildest and most gigantic of the primitive epic fancies, there is no conception so colossal as the being who is both Zeus and Prometheus.

(TT, ch. 29)

[see also: Angels, Cross, Death, Evil, Ghosts, Jesus, Mary, Mass, Miracles, Original Sin, Resurrection, Sacramentalism, Saints, Satan & Demons, Sin, Transubstantiation, Trinitarianism]

Incense

It might well be asked, indeed, why any one accepting the Bethlehem tradition should object to golden or gilded ornament since the Magi themselves brought gold, why he should dislike incense in the church since incense was brought even to the stable.

(EM, II-4)

[see also: Asceticism, Ceremony, Confession, Faith, Martyrdom, Mass, Mysticism, Relics, Robes, Sabbath, Temptation]

Inquisition, The

Theologians used racks and thumbscrews just as they used thimbles and three-legged stools, because everybody else used them.

Christianity no more created the mediaeval tortures than it did the Chinese tortures; it inherited them from any empire as heathen as the Chinese.

(MM, ch. 34)

But most men, even in the last and worst days of the Inquisition, went to their graves without knowing any more about the thumbscrew than most American citizens know about the Third Degree, and much less than they know about the ceremonial of burning negroes alive.

(ROC, Epilogue)

To understand the Spanish Inquisition it would be necessary to discover two things that we have never dreamed of bothering about; what Spain was and what an Inquisition was.

(SF, ch. 2)

The Spanish Inquisition was not an institution that I specially admire, but it did act on some intelligible principles; I know what the principles were and I agree with a great many of them.

(ILN, "The Modern Censor," 3-23-29)

[see also: Crusades, "Dark Ages," Dogma (Catholic), Empires, Greeks, History, History (Church), Hypocrisy (of Christians), Middle Ages, Renaissance, Tolerance, Victorianism, War, War (and Christianity)]

Intelligentsia; Scholars; The Learned

As I have pointed out elsewhere in this book, the expert is more aristocratic than the aristocrat, because the aristocrat is only the man who lives well, while the expert is the man who knows better.

(H, ch. 16)

I think that you and I are quite justified in disagreeing with doctors, however extraordinary in their erudition, if they violate ordinary reason in their line of argument.

For I rebel against the man of learning when he suddenly, and in public, refuses to think.

But when learned men begin to use their reason, then I generally discover that they haven't got any.

(ILN, "Arguing With Erudition," 10-31-08)

One does not need any learning to say that a man was killed or that a man was raised from the dead.

One does not need to be an astronomer to say that a star fell from heaven; or a botanist to say that a fig tree withered; or a chemist to say that one had seen water turned to wine; or a surgeon to say that one has seen wounds in the hands of St. Francis.

(ILN, "Miracles and Scientific Method," 4-17-09)

The third class is that of the Professors or Intellectuals; sometimes described as the thoughtful people; and these are a blight and a desolation both to their families and also to mankind.

The Prigs rise above the people by refusing to understand them: by saying that all their dim, strange preferences are prejudices and superstitions.

The Prigs make the people feel stupid; the Poets make the people feel wiser than they could have imagined that they were.

The Prigs who despise the people are often loaded with lands and crowned.

In the House of Commons, for instance, there are quite a number of prigs, but comparatively few poets.

He has not sufficient finesse and sensitiveness to sympathize with the mob.

His only notion is coarsely to contradict it, to cut across it, in accordance with some egotistical plan of his own; to tell himself that, whatever the ignorant say, they are probably wrong.

He forgets that ignorance often has the exquisite intuitions of innocence.

(AD, ch. 23)

But the curious thing about the educated class is that exactly what it does not know is what it is talking about.

(UTO, "The Empire of the Ignorant")

Why is it that for the last two or three centuries the educated have been generally wrong and the uneducated relatively right?

What the educated man has generally done was to ram down everybody's throat some premature and priggish theory which he himself afterwards discovered to be wrong; so wrong that he himself generally recoiled from it and went staggering to the opposite extreme.

(ILN, "The Wisdom of the Ignorant," 8-9-24)

The professor can preach any sectarian idea, not in the name of a sect, but in the name of a science.

(ILN, "Compulsory Education and the Monkey Trial," 8-8-25)

And those who have been there will know what I mean when I say that, while there are stupid people everywhere, there is a particular minute and microcephalous idiocy which is only found in an intelligentsia.

I have sometimes fancied that, as chilly people like a warm room, silly people sometimes like a diffused atmosphere of intellectualism and long words.

(ILN, "The Defense of the Unconventional," 10-17-25)

So many people, especially learned people and even clever people, seem to be quite unable to see the upshot of a thing; or what the French call its reason of being.

(ILN, "The Point – Getting It and Missing It," 10-30-26)

I have frequently visited such societies, in the capacity of a common or normal fool, and I have almost always found there a few fools who were more fool-ish than I had imagined to be possible to man born of woman; people who had hardly enough brains to be called half-witted.

But it gave them a glow within to be in what they imagined to be the atmosphere of intellect; for they worshipped it like an unknown god.

Intelligence does exist even in the Intelligentsia.

Anyhow, it is in this intellectual world, with its many fools and few wits and fewer wise men, that there goes on perpetually a sort of ferment of fashionable revolt and negation.

(TT, ch. 6)

But a large section of the Intelligentsia seemed wholly devoid of Intelligence.

As was perhaps natural, those who pontificated most pompously were often the most windy and hollow.

(A, ch. 7)

[see also: Common Sense, Critics, Experts, Gentlemen, "Higher Culture," Humanitarianism, Man (Common), Prigs]

Inventions and Innovations

It is an obvious canon of justice and commonsense that we have no right to invent an entirely new process and then complain that the civilization to which we belong does not immediately take account of it.

We have no right merely to invent something very fast and then call everything else very slow.
(ILN, "Superstition and Modern Justice," 10-6-06)

But civilization is to be tested not so much by the dexterity of inventions as by the worth of what is invented.
(ILN, "America and Barbarism," 2-16-07)

Inventions have destroyed invention.
(OS, ch. 4)

[see also: Automobiles, Capitalism, Cities, Communications, Hustle & Bustle, Traffic]

Ireland

The tendency of that argument is to represent the Irish or the Celts as a strange and separate race, as a tribe of eccentrics in the modern world immersed in dim legends and fruitless dreams.

Its tendency is to exhibit the Irish as odd, because they see the fairies.

Its trend is to make the Irish seem weird and wild because they sing old songs and join in strange dances.

It is the English who are odd because they do not see the fairies.

It is the inhabitants of Kensington who are weird and wild because they do not sing old songs and join in strange dances.

In all this the Irish are simply an ordinary sensible nation, living the life of any other ordinary and sensible nation which has not been either sodden with smoke or oppressed by money-lenders, or otherwise corrupted with wealth and science.

It is not Ireland which is mad and mystic; it is Manchester which is mad and mystic, which is incredible, which is a wild exception among human things.

In the matter of visions, Ireland is more than a nation, it is a model nation.

(H, ch. 13)

But the Irish peasant also has qualities which are common to all peasants, and his nation has qualities that are common to all healthy nations.

The average autochthonous Irishman is close to patriotism because he is close to the earth; he is close to domesticity because he is close to the earth; he is close to doctrinal theology and elaborate ritual because he is close to the earth.

In short, he is close to the heavens because he is close to the earth.

I incline to think myself that the Catholic Church has added charity and gentleness to the virtues of a people which would otherwise have been too keen and contemptuous, too aristocratic.

                                    (GBS, "The Puritan")

[see also:America, Scotland]

Jargon and "Catchwords"

And never before, I should imagine, in the intellectual history of the world have words been used with so idiotic an indifference to their actual meaning.

The modern man who prides himself on looking the world in the face and seeing what it means does not look one single word in the face and see what that means.
(ILN, "New Religion and New Irreligion," 4-4-08)

There are a hundred improved means of communication, and there is nothing to communicate.
(ILN, "The Meaning of Travel," 10-2-26)

We cannot all play like Paderewski or think like Plato, but we should be a great deal nearer to it if we could forget these little tags of talk from the daily papers and the debating clubs, and start afresh, thinking for ourselves.
(ILN, "Thought Versus Slogans," 2-18-28)

I mean by trash something much more essential and psychological; I mean the tendency to get the mind itself stuffed with rubbish, in the sense of wordy expositions of anything or nothing; or phrases that are only the fragments of philosophies; of dead words used like talismans, like the dead hand.

In short, the cult of Trash is the contrary of the cult of Truth; it means using language, or even learning and literature, without any lively current of curiosity or purpose running in the direction of Truth.

I mean by trash a man talking through his hat, because it is a fashionable hat.

That is, I mean a man (or a woman) talking unconsciously and mechanically, but at the same time pompously and with the pride of being in the mode.
(ILN, "The Swamp of Trash," 7-6-29)

There are any number of phrases which everybody speaks and nobody hears.

There are any number of phrases which when they were used the first time may have meant something, and which are now used for the millionth time because they mean nothing.
(ILN, "The Art of Thinking," 8-31-29)

[see also: Euphemisms, Fiction, Language, Newspapers, Novels, Poetry, Stories, Vernacular, Writers]

Jesus Christ

Christ did not love humanity; He never said He loved humanity: He loved men.

(TWE, ch. 10)

Really, if Jesus of Nazareth was not Christ, He must have been Antichrist.

For orthodox theology has specially insisted that Christ was not a being apart from God and man, like an elf, nor yet a being half human and half not, like a centaur, but both things at once and both things thoroughly, very man and very God.

(O, ch. 6)

What he said was always unexpected; but it was always unexpectedly magnanimous and often unexpectedly moderate.

(EM, II-3)

[see also: Angels, Cross, Death, Evil, Ghosts, Incarnation, Mary, Mass, Miracles, Original Sin, Resurrection, Sacramentalism, Saints, Satan & Demons, Sin, Transubstantiation, Trinitarianism]

Jews and Judaism

In the same conversation a free-thinker, a friend of mine, blamed Christianity for despising Jews, and then despised it himself for being Jewish.

(O, ch. 6)

But with all their fine apprehensions, the Jews suffer from one heavy calamity; that of being a Chosen Race.

(NJ, ch. 2)

The old religious Jews do not welcome the new nationalist Jews; it would sometimes be hardly an exaggeration to say that one party stands for the religion without the nation, and the other for the nation without the religion.

There is no place for the Temple of Solomon but on the ruins of the Mosque of Omar.

There is no place for the nation of the Jews but in the country of the Arabs.

(NJ, ch. 6)

The Jews are not like other races; they remain as unique to everybody else as they are to themselves.

(NJ, ch. 9)

That the Jews should have some high place of dignity and ritual in Palestine, such as a great building like the Mosque of Omar, is certainly right and reasonable; for upon no theory can their historic connection be dismissed.

I think it is sophistry to say, as do some Anti-Semites, that the Jews have no more right there than the Jebusites.

(NJ, ch. 13)

[see also: Religion (Comparative)]

Language and Grammar

Some of the most enormous and idiotic developments of our modern thought and speech arise simply from not knowing the parts of speech and principles of language, which we once knew when we were children.

For most fundamental falsehoods are errors in language as well as in philosophy.
(ILN, "Adjectives, Nouns, and the Truth," 10-16-09)

There are some who actually like the Country dialects which State education is systematically destroying.
(AS, ch. 6)

[see also: Euphemisms, Fiction, Jargon, Newspapers, Novels, Poetry, Stories, Vernacular, Writers]

Law

In our legal method there is too much lawyer and too little law.

For we must never forget one fact, which we tend to forget nevertheless: that a fixed rule is the only protection of ordinary humanity against clever men – who are the natural enemies of humanity.

The law is our only barrier against lawyers.
                    (ILN, "Fancies and Facts," 9-22-06)

Solemnity and speciality are the redeeming points of law.

The best part of a barrister is his wig.

By far the most humane and genial part of any legal proceedings are the oaths and the ritual phrases.
          (ILN, "Solemnity and Ritual in the Law," 2-23-07)

In short, we do not get good laws to restrain bad people.

We get good people to restrain bad laws.
                                        (ATC, ch. 16)

No one suggests that we should examine the Judge as to his private life, his politics, and, above all, his enormous income.

No one demands that we should allow for the bias and habit of the lawyer; no one asks whether men do not get dusty from living in gowns, or wooly from living in wigs, as much as efts get slimy from living in ponds or fish get wet from living in the sea.

The witness is, normally speaking, the only reliable man in court.

The barristers are unreliable, avowedly and honestly unreliable: it is their duty to be unreliable.

The Judge is unreliable, as all human history proves, which is a mere tissue of the partialities, pious frauds, Government persecutions and hack butcheries of the hired Judge on the bench.
                    (ILN, "Miracles and Scientific Method," 4-17-09)

Our civilisation has decided, and very justly decided, that determining the guilt or innocence of men is a thing too important to be trusted to trained men.
                                        (TRE, ch. 11)

Law has become lawless; that is, it cannot see where laws should stop.
                                        (EUG, I-8)

We are always near the breaking-point when we care only for what is legal and nothing for what is lawful.
                    (ILN, "The New Immoral Philosophy," 9-21-29)

[see also: Anarchy, Aristocracy, Caesaropapism, Conservatism, Democracy, Government, Liberalism (Political),

Monarchy, Nationalism, Nazism, Patriotism, Politicians, Revolution, Socialism, Spain (Civil War), Tolerance, Voting]

Liberalism (Political)

The sort of prig who sneers at patriotism commonly calls himself a Liberal.
(ILN, "Certain Incongruities at Christmas," 12-22-23)

I am still a Liberal; it is only the Liberal Party that has disappeared.
(WEL, "The Case of Spain")

[see also: Anarchy, Aristocracy, Caesaropapism, Conservatism, Democracy, Government, Law, Monarchy, Nationalism, Nazism, Patriotism, Politicians, Revolution, Socialism, Spain (Civil War), Tolerance, Voting]

Liberalism (Theological)

On the contrary, they are keeping the form and altering the truth.

On the contrary, they cling convulsively to the antiquated world; but make it mean something entirely different.
(ILN, "The New Theology and Modern Thought,"
3-23-07)

Almost every contemporary proposal to bring freedom into the church is simply a proposal to bring tyranny into the world.

It means freeing that peculiar set of dogmas loosely called scientific, dogmas of monism, of pantheism, or of Arianism, or of necessity.

For some inconceivable cause a "broad" or "liberal" clergyman always means a man who wishes at least to diminish the number of miracles; it never means a man who wishes to increase that number.

(O, ch. 8)

I am quite ready to respect another man's faith; but it is too much to ask that I should respect his doubt, his worldly hesitations and fictions, his political bargain and make-believe.

(WWW, I-3)

In point of fact, they have kept some of the words and terminology, words like Peace and Righteousness and Love; but they make these words stand for an atmosphere utterly alien to Christendom; they keep the letter and lose the spirit.

(ILN, "Keeping the Spirit of Christmas," 12-26-25)

For I grew up in a world in which the Protestants, who had just proved that Rome did not believe the Bible, were excitedly discovering that they did not believe the Bible themselves.

(CCC, ch. 2)

But the idea is that men should lose their old notions while retaining their old names; that they should lose them and not know what they had lost.

(ILN, "A New Statement of Religion?," 6-9-28)

To tell the priest to throw away any theology and impress us with his personality, is exactly like telling the doctor to throw away physiology and merely hypnotise us with his glittering eye.

(ILN, "If I Were a Preacher," 1-19-29)

The peculiarity of the position is not that Claude has proclaimed himself an Infidel; but that Claude has proclaimed himself a Christian with a higher and more purely spiritual religion, which is too exalted to believe in any creeds or sacraments, but which does permit him to remain an ordinary respectable Anglican parson – or possibly even an Anglican bishop.

(ILN, "The Family of the Bright Young Things," 10-5-29)

So long as the writer employs vast and universal gestures of fellowship and hospitality to all those who are ready to abandon their religious beliefs, he is allowed to be as rude as he likes to all those who venture to retain them.

(TT, Introduction)

It shines with Pharisaical self-satisfaction, because there are no crimes committed for its creed and no creed to be the motive of its crimes.

(TT, ch. 7)

The man who picks out some part of Catholicism that happens to please him, or throws away some part that happens to puzzle him, does in fact produce, not only the queerest sort of result, but generally the very opposite result to what he intends.

(TT, ch. 30)

But I cannot understand why something which is unpopular because of what it means should become frightfully popular because it no longer means anything.

Nor would most people, indifferent to the Christian origin of Christian churches, waste their time in churches merely because they had ceased to be Christian.

Even supposing it were true that theology is unpopular, it does not follow that the absence of theology is popular.

And surely those who are so innocently confident of the attraction of merely negative religion might realize that a broad-minded parson can be as much of a bore about nothing as anybody can be about anything.

(ILN, "On Abolishing the Churches," 10-4-30)

But even the stink of decaying heathenism has not been so bad as the stink of decaying Christianity.

(WEL, "Sex and Property")

[see also: Agnosticism, Authority, Darwinism, Determinism, Hedonism, "Higher Criticism," Modernism, Physics (Modern), Pragmatism, Progress (Idea of), Rebellion, Science, Secularism, Skepticism, Utopias]

Life

One after another almost every one of the phenomena of the universe has been declared to be alone capable of making life worth living.

Books, love, business, religion, alcohol, abstract truth, private emotion, money, simplicity, mysticism, hard work, a life close to nature, a life close to Belgrave Square are every one of them passionately maintained by somebody to be so good that they redeem the evil of an otherwise indefensible world.

Thus while the world is almost always condemned in summary, it is always justified, and indeed extolled, in detail after detail.

(TWE, ch. 3)

Sensibility is the definition of life.

(H, ch. 5)

And this strangeness of life, this unexpected and even perverse element of things as they fall out, remains incurably interesting.

But life is always a novel.

But in order that life should be a story or romance to us, it is necessary that a great part of it, at any rate, should be settled for us without our permission.

The thing which keeps life romantic and full of fiery possibilities is the existence of these great plain limitations which force all of us to meet the things we do not like or do not expect.

(H, ch. 14)

Streets are not life, cities and civilisations are not life, faces even and voices are not life itself.

Life is within, and no man hath seen it at any time.
(CD, ch. 1)

The important thing in life is not to keep a steady system of pleasure and composure (which can be done quite well by hardening one's heart or thickening one's head), but to keep alive in oneself the immortal power of astonishment and laughter, and a kind of young reverence.
(ILN, "The Survival of Christmas," 1-11-08)

The real basis of life is not scientific; the strongest basis of life is sentimental.
(ILN, "The Wrong Books at Christmas," 1-9-09)

For the perplexity of life arises from there being too many interesting things in it for us to be interested properly in any of them; what we call its triviality is really the tag-ends of numberless tales; ordinary and unmeaning existence is like ten thousand thrilling detective stories mixed up with a spoon.
(TRE, ch. 3)

The principle is this: that in everything worth having, even in every pleasure, there is a point of pain or tedium that must be survived, so that the pleasure may revive and endure.

In everything on this earth that is worth doing, there is a stage when no one would do it, except for necessity or honor.
(WWW, I-7)

Life in itself is not a ladder; it is a see-saw.
(WEL, "When the World Turned Back")

The aim of life is appreciation; there is no sense in not appreciating things; and there is no sense in having more of them if you have less appreciation of them.
(A, ch. 16)

[see also: Alcohol, Artificiality, Boredom, Dancing, Dreams, Efficiency, Happiness, Heroes, Rest, Sentimentalism, Taste, Travel, Vulgarity, Walking, Wallpaper, Weather, Work]

Life, Origin Of

The original rising of life from the lifeless is as strange as a rising from the dead.
(ILN, "Mr Edison's New Argument From Design,"
5-3-24)

[see also: Creation, Darwinism, Materialism, Medicine (Alternative), Physics (Modern), Science, Science (and Religion), Theism]

Madness

Every one who has had the misfortune to talk with people in the heart or on the edge of mental disorder, knows that their most sinister quality is a horrible clarity of detail; a connecting of one thing with another in a map more elaborate than a maze.

The madman is the man who has lost everything except his reason.

(O, ch. 2)

[see also: Despair, Fanatics, Moods, Optimism, Pessimism, Resignation, Suicide]

Man

If he is not the image of God, then he is a disease of the dust.

If it is not true that a divine being fell, then we can only say that one of the animals went entirely off its head.

Man is always something worse or something better than the animal; and a mere argument from animal perfection never touches him at all.
(ILN, "Alcohol, Drunkenness, and Drinking," 4-20-07)

Man was a statue of God walking about the garden.
(O, ch. 6)

If you wish to realise how fearfully and wonderfully God's image is made, stand on one leg.
(TRE, ch. 7)

Man is not merely an evolution but rather a revolution.
(ILN, "Our Intellectual Novelists," 7-10-26)

All that talk about the divinity and dignity of the human body is stolen from theology, and is quite meaningless without theology.
(ILN, "The Trouble With Our Pagans," 9-13-30)

[see also: Abortion, Animal Rights, Anthropology, Ceremony, Customs, Environment, Environmentalism, Euthanasia, Man (Common), Man (Smallness of), Men (Great), Morality, Nationality, Nature, Sociology]

Man, Common

Of course, this shrinking from the brutal vivacity and brutal variety of common men is a perfectly reasonable and excusable thing as long as it does not pretend to any point of superiority.

It is when it calls itself aristocracy or aestheticism or a superiority to the bourgeoisie that its inherent weakness has in justice to be pointed out.

(H, ch. 14)

I know that most modern writers (especially revolutionary writers) maintain that the populace is always wrong.

But if you want ideals, it is immeasurably better to go to the mob.

The bulk of a people always has a fairly sane and honourable philosophy.

(ILN, "On Punishing the Rich," 8-22-08)

But there is something psychologically Christian about the idea of seeking for the opinion of the obscure rather than taking the obvious course of accepting the opinion of the prominent.

(O, ch. 7)

Things are not altered so quickly or completely by common people as they are by fashionable people.

If you wish to find the past preserved, follow the million feet of the crowd.

(TRE, ch. 33)

The first kind of people are People; they are the largest and probably the most valuable class.

We owe to this class the chairs we sit down on, the
clothes we wear, the houses we live in; and, indeed (when
we come to think of it), we probably belong to this class
ourselves.

The class called People (to which you and I, with no
little pride, attach ourselves) has certain casual, yet profound, assumptions, which are called "commonplaces,"
as that children are charming, or that twilight is sad
and sentimental, or that one man fighting three is a fine
sight.

(AD, ch. 23)

Thus, to appreciate the virtues of the mob one must
either be on a level with it (as I am) or be really high up,
like the saints.

· (AD, ch. 32)

Now in these primary things in which the old religion
trusted a man, the new philosophy utterly distrusts a man

It is this profound scepticism about the common
man that is the common point in the most contradictory
elements of modern thought.

(OS, ch. 6)

On thousands of things the men who talk most of the
common bond are ignorant of what is really common.

(ILN, "The Spirit of Europe," 1-11-30)

Progress has been merely the persecution of the Common Man.

(CM, "The Common Man")

[see also: Common Sense, Critics, Experts, Gentlemen, "Higher Culture," Humanitarianism, Intelligentsia, Prigs]

Man, "Smallness" Of

It is quite futile to argue that man is small compared to the cosmos; for man was always small compared to the nearest tree.

(O, ch. 4)

No; that argument about man looking mean and trivial in the face of the physical universe has never terrified me at all, because it is a merely sentimental argument, and not a rational one in any sense or degree.

But if we are seriously debating whether a man is the moral center of this world, then he is no more morally dwarfed by the fact that his is not the largest star than by the fact that he is not the largest mammal.

Unless it can be maintained *a priori* that Providence must put the largest soul in the largest body, and must make the physical and moral center the same, "the vertigo of the infinite" has no more spiritual value than the vertigo of a ladder or the vertigo of a balloon.

(ILN, "Man in the Cosmos," 2-19-10)

Marriage

A man and a woman cannot live together without having against each other a kind of everlasting joke.

Each has discovered that the other is a fool, but a great fool.

This largeness, this grossness and gorgeousness of folly is the thing which we all find about those with whom we are in intimate contact; and it is the one enduring basis of affection, and even of respect.

(CD, ch. 10)

As long as a marriage is founded on a good solid incompatibility, that marriage has a fair chance of continuing to be a happy marriage, and even a romance.

(ILN, "Incompatibility in Marriage," 9-19-08)

The man and the woman are one flesh—yes, even when they are not one spirit.

I have known many happy marriages, but never a compatible one.

The whole aim of marriage is to fight through and survive the instant when incompatibility becomes unquestionable.

(WWW, I-7)

If ever monogamy is abandoned in practice, it will linger in legend and in literature.

(FVF, ch. 12)

How marriage can be a sacrament if sex is a sin, or why it is the Catholics who are in favour of birth and their foes who are in favour of birth-control, I will leave the critic to worry out for himself.

(STA, ch. 4)

To put the matter in one metaphor, the sexes are two stubborn pieces of iron; if they are to be welded together, it must be while they are red-hot.

(CM, "Two Stubborn Pieces of Iron")

[see also: Birth Control, Chivalry, Contraception, Divorce, Eugenics, Family, Feminism, Fidelity, Gender Differences, Home, Motherhood, Mothers-in-Law, Sexuality, Wives]

Martyrdom

A martyr is a man who cares so much for something outside him, that he forgets his own personal life.

(O, ch. 5)

[see also: Asceticism, Confession, Faith, Incense, Mysticism, Relics, Robes, Sabbath, Saints, Temptation]

Mary, Blessed Virgin

But I know that I shall never exhaust the profundity of that unfathomable paradox which is defined so defiantly in the very title of the Mother of God.

(TT, ch. 29)

That strange mania against Mariolatry; that mad vigilance that watches for the first faint signs of the cult of Mary as for the spots of a plague; that apparently presumes her to be perpetually and secretly encroaching upon the prerogatives of Christ; that logically infers from a mere glimpse of the blue robe the presence of the Scarlet Woman—all that I have never felt or known or understood, even as a child; nor did those who had the care of my childhood.

(WEL, "Mary and the Convert")

[see also: Angels, Cross, Death, Evil, Ghosts, Incarnation, Jesus, Mass, Miracles, Original Sin, Resurrection, Sacramentalism, Saints, Satan & Demons, Sin, Transubstantiation, Trinitarianism]

Mass, The

When the critic in question, or a thousand other critics like him, say that we are only required to make a material or mechanical attendance at Mass, he says something which is *not* true about the ordinary Catholic in his feelings about the Catholic Sacraments.

(TT, ch. 13)

To exalt the Mass is to enter into a magnificent world of metaphysical ideas, illuminating all the relations of matter and mind, of flesh and spirit, of the most impersonal abstractions as well as the most personal affections.

(TT, ch. 29)

[see also: Angels, Cross, Death, Evil, Ghosts, Incarnation, Incense, Jesus, Mary, Miracles, Original Sin, Resurrection, Sacramentalism, Saints, Satan & Demons, Sin, Transubstantiation, Trinitarianism]

Materialism (Scientific and Philosophical)

I have come into the country where men do definitely believe that the waving of the trees makes the wind.

That is to say, they believe that the material circumstances, however black and twisted, are more important than the spiritual realities, however powerful and pure.

By perpetually talking about environment and visible things, by perpetually talking about economics and physical necessity, painting and keeping repainted a perpetual picture of iron machinery and merciless engines, of rails of steel, and of towers of stone, modern materialism at last produces this tremendous impression in which the truth is stated upside down.

(TRE, ch. 14)

It was the materialists who destroyed materialism, merely by studying matter.

We have been accused of hostility to the scientist, when we are merely hostile to the materialist.

The venerable Victorian materialist wanted the world to grow more and more scientific; but only on the strict condition that the science should grow more and more materialistic.

(ILN, "Old Science and New Science," 5-9-31)

If fifty years hence the electron is as entirely exploded as the atom, it will not affect us; for we have never founded our philosophy on the electron any more than on the atom.

(WEL, "The Collapse of Materialism")

[see also: Agnosticism, Atheism, Authority, Creation, Darwinism, Determinism, Life (Origin of), Modernism, Physics (Modern), Pragmatism, Progress (Idea of), Rebellion, Science, Science (and Religion), Secularism, Skepticism, Utopias]

Medicine, Alternative

The argument used by professional men of science that what they call quack remedies are superstitions is really an argument in a circle.

It amounts to this, that the herbs used by an old woman are untrustworthy because she is superstitious; and she is superstitious because she believes in such herbs.

(ILN, "Charlatans and Quacks," 2-15-08)

[see also: Philosophy, Science]

Men, Great

One of the actual and certain consequences of the idea that all men are equal is immediately to produce very great men.

But the real great man is the man who makes every man feel great.

It has often been said, very truly, that religion is the thing that makes the ordinary man feel extraordinary; it is an equally important truth that religion is the thing that makes the extraordinary man feel ordinary.

(CD, ch. 1)

[see also: Man]

Mercy

Mercy does not mean not being cruel or sparing people revenge or punishment; it means a plain and positive thing like the sun, which one has either seen or not seen.

(TRE, ch. 2)

Middle Ages; Mediaevalism

But there is something odd in the fact that when we reproduce the Middle Ages it is always some such rough and half-grotesque part of them that we reproduce.

But why is it that we mainly remember the Middle Ages by absurd things?

Few modern people know what a mass of illuminating philosophy, delicate metaphysics, clear and dignified social morality exists in the serious scholastic writers of mediaeval times.

But we seem to have grasped somehow that the ruder and more clownish elements in the Middle Ages have a human and poetical interest.

We are delighted to know about the ignorance of mediaevalism; we are contented to be ignorant about its knowledge.

We forget that Parliaments are mediaeval, that all our Universities are mediaeval, that city corporations are mediaeval, that gunpowder and printing are mediaeval, that half the things by which we now live, and to which we look for progress, are mediaeval.

(ILN, "The True Middle Ages," 7-14-06)

It was perhaps the one real age of progress in all history.

Men have seldom moved with such rapidity and such unity from barbarism to civilisation as they did from the end of the Dark Ages to the times of the universities and the parliaments, the cathedrals and the guilds.

(NJ, ch. 12)

The medieval world did not talk about Plato and Cicero as fools occupied with futilities; yet that is exactly how a more modern world talked of the philosophy of Aquinas and sometimes even of the purely philosophic parts of Dante.

(SL, "The Camp and the Cathedral" [1922])

I have never maintained that mediaeval things were all good; it was the bigots who maintained that mediaeval things were all bad.

(ILN, "Mediaeval Robber Barons and Other Myths," 5-26-23)

They started by saying that mediaeval life was utterly miserable; they find out that it was frequently cheerful; so they make an attempt to represent its cheerfulness as a wild revolt that demonstrates its misery.

Every impossibility is possible, except the possibility that the whole assumption about the Middle Ages is wrong.

(ILN, "More Myths, Mediaeval and Victorian," 6-2-23)

These mediaeval things were good not because they were mediaeval, but because they were moral; they took rather more seriously certain permanent ideals of justice and mercy.

(ILN, "The Old-Fashioned and the New-Fangled," 7-28-23)

The thirteenth century was certainly a progressive period; perhaps the only really progressive period in human history.

But it can truly be called progressive precisely because its progress was very orderly.

It is really and truly an example of an epoch of reforms without revolutions.

(SF, ch. 4)

It was the enemies of mediaevalism who made up the romance about castles and tournaments, and represented that such romantic ruins and rumours were all that could be got out of mediaeval culture.

(ILN, "Cobbett's View of History," 7-4-25)

The mediaeval man thought in terms of the Thesis, where the modern man thinks in terms of the Essay.

(ILN, "On the Essay," 2-16-29)

If the mediaeval religion had really been such a silly superstition as some of its simpler enemies represent, it quite certainly would have been swallowed up for ever in such an earthquake of enlightenment as the great Renaissance.

The fact that the vision of a superb and many-sided human culture did not disturb the fundamental ideas of these late mediaeval Christians has a simple explanation: that the ideas are true.

(ILN, "The Truth of Mediaeval Times," 1-18-30)

I need not say that half the great educational foundations, not only Oxford and Cambridge, but Glasgow and Paris, are relics of mediaevalism.

(AIS, ch. 3)

[see also: Cathedrals, Chivalry, Christianity, Church (Catholic), Crusades, "Dark Ages", Development (Doctrinal), Empires, Fairy Tales, Guilds, History, History (Church), Hypocrisy (of Christians), Inquisition, Mythology, Orthodoxy, Philosophy, Reason and Logic, Orthodoxy, Renaissance, Romanticism]

Miracles

If a miracle is not exceptional, it is not even miraculous.

(ILN, "Taking Reason by the Right End," 11-7-08)

The reason is that a Free Thinker does not mean a man who thinks freely; a Free Thinker means a man who is not allowed to think that miracles happen.

(ILN, "The Proper Idea of Property," 11-14-08)

But the materialist is not allowed to admit into his spotless machine the slightest speck of spiritualism or miracle.

(O, ch. 2)

But my belief that miracles have happened in human history is not a mystical belief at all; I believe in them upon human evidences as I do in the discovery of America.

The disbelievers in miracles deny them (rightly or wrongly) because they have a doctrine against them.

The sceptic always takes one of the two positions; either an ordinary man need not be believed, or an extraordinary event must not be believed.

(O, ch. 9)

The rest is all cant and repetition and arguing in a circle; all the baseless dogmatism about science forbidding men to believe in miracles; as if *science* could forbid men to believe in something which science does not profess to investigate.

Science is the study of the admitted laws of existence; it cannot prove a universal negative about whether those laws could ever be suspended by something admittedly above them.

(TT, ch. 28)

As a matter of fact, we are the freer of the two; as there is scarcely any evidence, natural or preternatural, that cannot be accepted as fitting into our system somewhere; whereas the materialist cannot fit the most minute miracle into his system anywhere.

(TT, ch. 30)

[see also: Agnosticism, Angels, Cross, Death, Evil, Ghosts, Incarnation, Jesus, Liberalism (Religious), Mary, Materialism, Miracles, Original Sin, Physics (Modern), Resurrection, Sacramentalism, Saints, Satan & Demons, Science, Sin, Skepticism, Transubstantiation, Trinitarianism]

Modernism

It is incomprehensible to me that any thinker can calmly call himself a modernist; he might as well call himself a Thursdayite.

The real objection to modernism is simply that it is a form of snobbishness.

It is an attempt to crush a rational opponent not by reason, but by some mystery of superiority, by hinting that one is specially up to date or particularly "in the know."

To introduce into philosophical discussions a sneer at a creed's antiquity is like introducing a sneer at a lady's age.

(ATC, ch. 1)

The modern young man will never change his environment; for he will always change his mind.

(O, ch. 7)

A modern thinker not only will not state his own opinion in clear, straightforward English, but he is hideously affronted if you do it for him.

(ILN, "Being True to Oneself," 8-14-09)

The modern man is more like a traveller who has forgotten the name of his destination, and has to go back whence he came, even to find out where he is going.

(NJ, ch. 1)

It fails in the quality that is truly called distinction; and, being incapable of distinction, it falls back on generalisation.

(ILN, "The Effort of Distinction," 1-6-23)

It is the beginning of all true criticism of our time to realize that it has really nothing to say, at the very moment, when it has invented so tremendous a trumpet for saying it.

(ILN, "A Proper View of Machines," 2-10-23)

They move about in a mesmerized and mechanical condition, talking and thinking merely on the authority of somebody who is not an authority.

(ILN, "Twilight Sleep and the Breakdown of Reason,"
11-2-29)

All this that calls itself Modern Thought is a series of false starts and belated stoppages.

It starts by believing in nothing, and it ends by getting nowhere.
        (ILN, "The Modern Recoil From the Modern," 11-9-29)

They come in at the end of every controversy and
know nothing of where it began or what it is all about.
                                            (TT, ch. 5)

The fact that stupidity has become stale to the read-
ers does not seem to prevent its being eternally fresh to
the writers.
            (ILN, "The Guilt of the Churches," 7-26-30)

We talk, by a sort of habit, about Modern Thought,
forgetting the familiar fact that moderns do not think.

They only feel, and that is why they are so much
stronger in fiction than in facts; why their novels are so
much better than their newspapers.
        (ILN, "The Trouble With Our Pagans," 9-13-30)

But when it comes to anything like a strain on the
intellect as such, I think that most modern people are
much stupider than those in the age of my father, and
probably very much stupider than those in the age of my
grandfather.

The minds of our fathers may have been occupied in
futile and pedantic hair-splitting, but their minds really
were capable of splitting a hair.
        (ILN, "The Laziness of the Modern Intellect," 10-11-30)

For the Modern Mind is not at all accustomed to making up its mind.

(WEL, "The Well and the Shallows")

But, alas, Mr. Shaw is a true Modernist in the fact that he cannot complete even his own argument, for fear it should end by proving something.

(WEL, "The Scripture Reader")

[see also: Agnosticism, Atheism, Authority, Darwinism, Determinism, Hedonism, Liberalism (Theological), Materialism, Physics (Modern), Pragmatism, Progress (Idea of), Rebellion, Science, Secularism, Skepticism, Utopias]

Monarchy; Divine Right of Kings

Thomas More died the death of a traitor for defying absolute monarchy; in the strict sense of treating monarchy as an absolute.

In that form it is now regarded as an old superstition; but it has already reappeared as a very new superstition, in the form of the Divine Right of Dictators.

And it is typical of all Catholic thought that men died in torments, not because their foes "spoke all false"; but simply because they would not give an unreasonable reverence where they were perfectly prepared to give a reasonable respect.

(WEL, "St. Thomas More")

[see also: Anarchy, Aristocracy, Caesaropapism, Conservatism, Democracy, Government, Law, Liberalism

(Political), Nationalism, Nazism, Patriotism, Politicians, Revolution, Socialism, Spain (Civil War), Tolerance, Voting]

Moods

No one worth calling a man allows his moods to change his convictions; but it is by moods that we understand other men's convictions.

(AD, ch. 19)

[see also: Despair, Fanatics, Madness, Optimism, Pessimism, Resignation, Suicide]

Morality

The act of defending any of the cardinal virtues has to-day all the exhilaration of a vice.

(DEF, ch. 12)

Morality did not begin by one man saying to another, "I will not hit you if you do not hit me"; there is no trace of such a transaction.

(O, ch. 5)

Paganism declared that virtue was in a balance; Christianity declared it was in a conflict: the collision of two passions apparently opposite.

(O, ch. 6)

Now, the word Ethics is already a nuisance to God and man; but its permanent defence and its occasional necessity is that it stands for conduct considered statically as a science, whereas morality (or moralitude) stands for conduct considered actively as a choice.

(ILN, "Modern Jargon," 6-12-09)

It seems to me that the mass of men do agree on the mass of morality, but differ disastrously about the proportions of it.

The difference between men is not in what merits they confess, but what merits they emphasise.

Men do not differ much about what things they will call evils; they differ enormously about what evils they will call excusable.

What men fight each other about is the question of which are the venial and which are the mortal sins.

(ILN, "The Proper Emphasis in Morality," 10-23-09)

Cleanliness is not next to godliness nowadays, for cleanliness is made essential and godliness is regarded as an offence.

(TRE, ch. 10)

The romance of conscience has been dried up into the science of ethics; which may well be called decency for decency's sake, decency unborn of cosmic energies and barren of artistic flower.

(WWW, III-2)

The trend of the new time, in very varying degrees, was tending to undermine, not merely the Christian demonology, not merely the Christian theology, not merely the Christian religion, but definitely the Christian ethical ideal, which had seemed to the great agnostic as secure as the stars.

(NJ, ch. 9)

And what is the answer, on the lines of this evolutionary and ever-changing morality, to anybody who chooses to say that anything will be considered moral in the future?

(ILN, "The Debate on Censorship, Continued," 3-31-28)

The proportions differ in practice; the ethical expression differs in emphasis; but virtue is virtue and vice is vice, in all ages and for all people, except a few lunatics.

(ILN, "On Fundamental Morality," 12-1-28)

Now, the trouble with nearly all modern discussions of these moral questions is not so much that they are immoral as that they are inconsistent.

(ILN, "The Attack on Impuritan Literature," 3-30-29)

If there are only Ten Commandments, it means that there are only ten things forbidden; and that means that there are ten million things that are not forbidden.

(AIS, ch. 13)

[see also: Abortion, Animal Rights, Casuistry, Charity, Compassion, Conscience, Courage, Decadence, Divorce, Despair, Ego, Environmentalism, Euthanasia, Fidelity, Hedonism, Hope, Hospitality, Humility, Man, Mercy, Pride, Self (Love of), Sexuality, Sincerity, Temper, "Values," Vegetarianism, Vows, Will]

Motherhood

For the fact is that we all know perfectly well that it was the best thing for all of us to be brought up by women, and by women alone.

(ILN, "Female Suffrage and the New Theology,"
3-16-07)

Two gigantic facts of nature fixed it thus: first, that the woman who frequently fulfilled her functions literally could not be specially prominent in experiment and adventure; and second, that the same natural operation surrounded her with very young children, who require to be taught not so much anything as everything.

Babies need not to be taught a trade, but to be introduced to a world.

To put the matter shortly, woman is generally shut up in a house with a human being at the time when he asks all the questions that there are, and some that there aren't.

But when people begin to talk about this domestic duty as not merely difficult but trivial and dreary, I simply give up the question.

(WWW, III-3)

Here and there we read of a girl brought up like a tom-boy; but every boy is brought up like a tame girl.

(WWW, III-10)

The point about the "half-time job" of motherhood is that it is at least one of the jobs that can be regarded as a whole, and almost as an end in itself.

(ILN, "Women in the Workplace—and at Home," 12-18-26)

The mother can bring up the child without choosing a religion for him, but not without choosing an environment for him.

(ILN, "Thought Versus Slogans," 2-18-28)

[see also: Abortion, Birth Control, Contraception, Divorce, Family, Feminism, Gender Differences, Home, Marriage, Motherhood, Mothers-in-Law, Sexuality, Wives]

Mothers-in-Law

Or to take another obvious instance: the jokes about a mother-in-law are scarcely delicate, but the problem of a mother-in-law is extremely delicate.

She is a mystical blend of two inconsistent things— law and a mother.

The nearest statement of the problem perhaps is this: it is not that a mother-in-law must be nasty, but that she must be very nice.

(WWW, II-2)

[see also: Family, Feminism, Home, Marriage, Motherhood, Sexuality, Wives]

Mysticism

The ordinary man has always been sane because the ordinary man has always been a mystic.

The whole secret of mysticism is this: that man can understand everything by the help of what he does not understand.

(O, ch. 2)

The wildest mystic uses his reason at some stage; if it be only by reasoning against reason.

(SL, "Anti-Religious Thought in the 18th Century"
[1926])

[see also: Asceticism, Confession, Faith, Incense, Martyrdom, Relics, Robes, Sabbath, Temptation]

Mythology, Fable, and Folklore

Every single practical and triumphant thing in this world has begun, not with an accuracy, but with a legend.

These dim, gigantic fables are the origins of all practical things.

(AWD, "For Persons of the Name of Smith" [1902])

Fable is, generally speaking, far more accurate than fact, for fable describes a man as he was to his own age, fact describes him as he is to a handful of inconsiderable antiquarians many centuries after.

(VT, ch. 14)

Folk-lore means that the soul is sane, but that the universe is wild and full of marvels.

(TRE, ch. 16)

Nearly all the fundamental facts of mankind are to be found in its fables.

(ILN, "The Bonds of Love," 7-2-10)

But neither can they leave a legend alone; though it is the essence of a legend to be vague.

(AD, ch. 15)

There can be no good fable with human beings in it.

Fables repose upon quite the opposite idea: that' everything is itself, and will in any case speak for itself.

This is the immortal justification of the Fable; that we could not teach the plainest truths so simply without turning men into chessmen.

There is every type and time of fable; but there is only one moral to the fable; because there is only one moral to everything.

(SL, "Aesop's Fables" [1912])

All the most subtle truths of literature are to be found in legend.

(FVF, ch. 12)

Modern men are not allowed to have any history; but at least nothing can prevent men from having legends.

(FVF, ch. 23)

Very deep things in our nature, some dim sense of the dependence of great things upon small, some dark suggestion that the things nearest to us stretch far beyond our power, some sacramental feeling of the magic in material substances, and many more emotions past fading out, are in an idea like that of the external soul.

It is the voice of a dreamer and an idealist crying, 'Why cannot these things be?'

(EM, I-5)

A void was made by the vanishing of the whole mythology of mankind, which would have asphyxiated like a vacuum if it had not been filled with theology.

(EM, I-8)

They all refer back to these ancient unfathomable wells which go down deeper than the reason into the very roots of the world, but contain the springs that refresh the reason and keep it active for ever.

(AIS, ch. 25)

Mythology is simply believing whatever you can imagine.

(AS, ch. 2)

[see also: Adventure, Children, Fairy Tales, Imagination, Romanticism, Stories, Wonder]

Nationalism

All good men are international.

Nearly all bad men are cosmopolitan.

If we are to be international we must be national.
(ATC, ch. 9)

[see also: Anarchy, Aristocracy, Caesaropapism, Conservatism, Democracy, Government, Law, Liberalism (Political), Monarchy, Nazism, Patriotism, Politicians, Revolution, Socialism, Spain (Civil War), Tolerance, Voting]

Nationality

Nationality exists, and has nothing in the world to do with race.

Nationality is a thing like a church or a secret society; it is a product of the human soul and will; it is a spiritual product.

(H, ch. 13)

It will generally be found, I think, that the more a man really appreciates and admires the soul of another people the less he will attempt to imitate it; he will be conscious that there is something in it too deep and too unmanageable to imitate.

(ATC, ch. 9)

[see also: Anthropology, Ceremony, Compartmentalization, Customs, Environment, Man, Man (Smallness of), Nationalism, Patriotism, Sociology]

Nature

The superficial impression of the world is by far the deepest.

What we really feel, naturally and casually, about the look of skies and trees and the face of friends, that and that alone will almost certainly remain our vital philosophy to our dying day.

(TWE, ch. 12)

Thoreau could enjoy the sunrise without a cup of coffee.

Nature can be enjoyed without even the most natural luxuries.

(H, ch. 7)

Barbarism means the worship of Nature; and in recent poetry, science, and philosophy there has been too much of the worship of Nature.

(ILN, "Europeans and Barbarians," 8-18-06)

There is no equality in nature; also there is no inequality in nature.

The essence of all pantheism, evolutionism, and modern cosmic religion is really in this proposition: that Nature is our mother.

The main point of Christianity was this: that Nature is not our mother: Nature is our sister.

To St. Francis, Nature is a sister, and even a younger sister: a little, dancing sister, to be laughed at as well as loved.

(O, ch. 7)

On bright blue days I do not want anything to happen; the world is complete and beautiful, a thing for contemplation.

(TRE, ch. 3)

Around me in that emerald twilight were trunks of trees of every plain or twisted type; it was like a chapel supported on columns of every earthly and unearthly style of architecture.

For the meaning of woods is the combination of energy with complexity.

A forest is not in the least rude or barbarous; it is only dense with delicacy.

(TRE, ch. 21)

In other words, the natural mystic does know that there is something there; something behind the clouds or within the trees; but he believes that the pursuit of beauty is the way to find it; that imagination is a sort of incantation that can call it up.

The poet feels the mystery of a particular forest; not of the science of afforestation or the department of woods and forests.

(EM, I-5)

Poets, even Pagans, can only directly believe in Nature if they indirectly believe in God; if the second idea should really fade, the first is bound to follow sooner or later; and, merely out of a sad respect for human logic, I wish it had been sooner.

Of course a man might have an almost animal appreciation of certain accidents of form or colour in a rock or a pool, as in a rag-bag or a dustbin; but that is not what the great poets or the great pagans meant by mysteries of Nature or the inspiration of the elemental powers.

That is the first note; that this common human mysticism about the dust or the dandelion or the daylight or the daily life of man does depend, and always did depend on theology, if it dealt at all in thought.

(A, ch. 16)

[see also: Creation, Pantheism, Poetry, Wonder]

Nazism

He is swift to shed innocent blood; he really has a certain technique in the matter of murdering other people; and the prospect of this sport alone can move him to an animation that is almost human.

Hitler really killed quite a creditable number of people for one week-end holiday; and the assassination of Dollfuss did show some touch of that efficiency, which the Nazis once promised to display in other fields of activity.

This is simply that very old remembrance of our race; the barbarian invasion.

It is the centre of our civilisation in peril; it is the blow of the barbarian when for once, in his blindness, he happens to aim at the heart.

(WEL, "Austria")

But I wonder if it is much truer to call Hitler a Catholic than to call Bertrand Russell an Anglo-Catholic.

In fact, the movement began before the Great War; before the Franco-Prussian War; and has its origins far back in history, in the fact that the Protestant edges of Germany only partly emerged from barbarism and soon relapsed into paganism.

The racial pride of Hitlerism is of the Reformation by twenty tests; because it divides Christendom and makes all such divisions deeper; because it is fatalistic, like Calvinism, and makes superiority depend not upon choice but only on being of the chosen; because it is Caesaro-Papist, putting the State above the Church, as in the claim of Henry VIII; because it is immoral, being an innovator of morals touching things like Eugenics and Sterility; because it is subjective, in suiting the primal fact to the personal fancy, as in asking for a German God, or saying that the Catholic revelation does not suit the German temper; as if I were to say that the Solar System does not suit the Chestertonian taste.

(WEL, "Where is the Paradox?")

[see also: Anarchy, Aristocracy, Caesaropapism, Conservatism, Democracy, Government, Law, Liberalism (Political), Monarchy, Nationalism, Patriotism, Politicians, Revolution, Socialism, Spain (Civil War), Tolerance, Voting]

Neighbors

What we dread about our neighbours, in short, is not the narrowness of their horizon, but their superb tendency to broaden it.

But we have to love our neighbour because he is there—a much more alarming reason for a much more serious operation.

He is the sample of humanity which is actually given us.

(H, ch. 14)

The Bible tells us to love our neighbours, and also to love our enemies; probably because they are generally the same people.

(ILN, "The Man Next Door," 7-16-10)

[see also: Cliques, Conversation, Friendship, Silent Types, Singing, Talkers]

Newspapers; Journalism; the Press; Media Bias

It may or may not be true that man's great use for language is to conceal his thoughts; but I suppose that we should all agree to the somewhat analogous proposition that the one great use of newspapers is to suppress news.

(ILN, "The Lies of Journalism," 3-2-07)

At present, it is not we that silence the Press; it is the Press that silences us.

It is not a case of the Commonwealth settling how much the editors shall say; it is a case of the editors settling how much the Commonwealth shall know.

(ILN, "Censoring the Press," 10-19-07)

But the modern editor regards himself far too much as a kind of original artist, who can select and suppress facts with the arbitrary ease of a poet or a caricaturist.

(ILN, "The Faults of the Press," 10-26-07)

But I have come to the conclusion that if you never believe the Press and if you always believe private gossip (within reason) you will probably be right.

The frivolous chatter is now all in public journalism.
(ILN, "Gossip and Public Journalism," 2-1-08)

The curse of all journalism, but especially of that yellow journalism which is the shame of our profession, is that we think ourselves cleverer than the people for whom we write, whereas, in fact, we are generally even stupider.

For the journalist, having grown accustomed to talking down to the public, commonly talks too low at last, and becomes merely barbaric and unintelligible.
(ATC, ch. 20)

They are, by the nature of the case, the hobbies of a few rich men.

We have a censorship by the press.

The chieftain chosen to be the friend of the people becomes the enemy of the people; the newspaper started to tell the truth now exists to prevent the truth being told.
(O, ch. 7)

It is by this time practically quite impossible to get the truth out of newspapers, even the honest newspapers.
(ILN, "Truth in the Newspapers," 1-23-09)

The new method of journalism is to offer so many comments or, at least, secondary circumstances that there is actually no room left for the original facts.

(ILN, "Distortions in the Press," 11-6-09)

It is a conspiracy of a very few millionaires, all sufficiently similar in type to agree on the limits of what this great nation (to which we belong) may know about itself and its friends and enemies.

The millionaire newspapers are vulgar and silly because the millionaires are vulgar and silly.

The official journalist for some time past has been both a bore and a liar; but it was impossible until lately to neglect his sheets of news altogether.

(UTO, "The Tyranny of Bad Journalism")

It seems impossible to exaggerate the evil that can be done by a corrupt and unscrupulous press.

But bad journalism does directly ruin the nation, considered as a nation; it acts on the corporate national will and sways the common national decision.

(FVF, ch. 9)

They will believe something passed by an editor they have never seen, employing a reporter they have never seen, printed in an office they have never visited, for reasons they will never know.

(ILN, "The Legends of My Youth," 9-18-26)

And the papers are shouting louder and louder like demagogues, merely because their hearers are growing more and more deaf.
(ILN, "On Reading, and Not Being Able To," 12-8-28)

There is really very good reason for saying that the Press in its present conditions is in danger of becoming an anomalous and anonymous bore.
(ILN, "Bowing Down to the New Religion," 4-13-29)

What I protest against is the prevailing fashion, in the Press and elsewhere, of parading all this perfectly natural indifference and ignorance as if it were a sort of impartiality.
(ILN, "Religion and the New Science," 4-12-30)

What I lament is the importance of head-lines and the unimportance of headwork; the eagerness to state a man's views, compared with the carelessness about whether his views are really stated, let alone whether they are really sound.
(ILN, "The Place of Mysticism," 5-24-30)

I am speaking of the widespread journalistic habit of retailing these scraps of anthropological or psychological gossip, to be read by "all thoughtful people"; that is, by all people thoughtless enough to accept them without a moment's thought.
(ILN, "Introverts and Extroverts," 7-19-30)

How do we manage to stagger on blinded by the blaze of wit and starry brilliancy, that is showered upon us like everlasting fireworks every day in the daily papers?

(WEL, "Shocking the Modernists")

In short, I only say that if dictators suppress newspapers, newspaper proprietors suppress news.

(WEL, "Why Protestants Prohibit")

[see also: Agnosticism, Atheism, Critics, Euphemisms, Experts, Fiction, "Higher Culture," Intelligentsia, Jargon, Language, Liberalism (Political), Modernism, Novels, Poetry, Prigs, Skepticism, Socialism, Stories, Vernacular, Writers]

Nonconformity (Christian)

The really courageous man is he who defies tyrannies young as the morning and superstitions fresh as the first flowers.

The only true free-thinker is he whose intellect is as much free from the future as from the past.

He cares as little for what will be as for what has been; he cares only for what ought to be.

I merely claim my choice of all the tools in the universe; and I shall not admit that any of them are blunted merely because they have been used.

(WWW, I-4)

[see also: Conformity, Fashions, Spirit of the Age (*Zeitgeist*)]

Novels, Modern

A good novel tells us the truth about its hero; but a bad novel tells us the truth about its author.

The more dishonest a book is as a book the more honest it is as a public document.

(H, ch. 15)

The problem of the modern novel is—what will a madman do with a dull world?

In the modern novels the hero is mad before the book begins, and suffers from the harsh steadiness and cruel sanity of the cosmos.

(TRE, ch. 16)

But supposing the man's tastes to be detached from the drama and from the kindred arts, he may prefer the reading of fiction; and he will have no difficulty in finding a popular novel about the doubts and difficulties of a good and kind clergyman slowly discovering that true religion consists of progress and social sympathy, with the assistance of a Modern Girl whose shingled hair and short skirts proclaim her indifference to all fine distinctions about who should be buried and who divorced; nor, probably, will the story fail to contain an American millionaire making vast financial consolidations, and certainly a yacht and possibly a Crown Prince.

(OS, ch. 4)

Novels are the great monument of the amazing credulity of the modern mind; for people believe them quite seriously, even though they do not pretend to be true.

People are minutely described as experiencing one idiotic passion after another, passions which they themselves recognise as idiotic, and which even their own wretched philosophy forbids them to regard as steps towards any end.

But the modern serious novel seriously denies that there is any goal.

They are driven back entirely on the microscopic description of these aimless appetites in themselves.

But modern philosophy has taken the life out of modern fiction.
(ILN, "The Sloppiness of the Modern Novel – and Modern Thought," 3-8-30)

[see also: Art and Artists, Fiction, Language, Jargon, Newspapers, Novels, Poetry, Stories, Writers]

Openmindedness

Mouths and minds were made to shut; they were made to open only in order to shut.

(ILN, "The History of Religions," 10-10-08)

[see also: Bigotry & Racism, Broadmindedness, Conspiratorialism, Dogmatism, Prejudice, Tolerance]

Optimism

The world is round, so round that the schools of optimism and pessimism have been arguing from the beginning whether it is the right way up.

(H, ch. 6)

The optimist is a better reformer than the pessimist; and the man who believes life to be excellent is the man who alters it most.

(CD, ch. 1)

Christianity was accused, at one and the same time, of being too optimistic about the universe and of being too pessimistic about the world.

(O, ch. 5)

St. Francis, in praising all good, could be a more shouting optimist than Walt Whitman.

(O, ch. 6)

One of the strangest things about the use of the word 'optimist' is that it is now so constantly used about the future.

(AWD, "What is Right With the World" [1910])

Of course, the chess-board that is our mortal battle-field can always be called black with white squares or white with black squares.

(ILN, "More Myths, Mediaeval and Victorian," 6-2-23)

The English love of believing that all is as it should be, the English optimism combined with the strong English imagination, is too much even for the obvious facts.

(HAT, ch. 11)

[see also: Despair, Fanatics, Madness, Moods, Pessimism, Resignation, Suicide]

Original Sin; Fall of Man

How could physical science find any traces of a moral fall?

Did he expect to find a fossil Eve with a fossil apple inside her?

The only thing we all know about that primary purity and innocence is that we have not got it.

(ILN, "Science and the Fall of Man," 9-28-07)

Certain new theologians dispute original sin, which is the only part of Christian theology which can really be proved.

(O, ch. 2)

God had written, not so much a poem, but rather a play; a play he had planned as perfect, but which had necessarily been left to human actors and stage-managers, who had since made a great mess of it.

(O, ch. 5)

If we wish to pull down the prosperous oppressor we cannot do it with the new doctrine of human perfectibility; we can do it with the old doctrine of Original Sin.

But Christianity preaches an obviously unattractive idea, such as original sin; but when we wait for its results, they are pathos and brotherhood, and a thunder of laughter and pity; for only with original sin we can at once pity the beggar and distrust the king.

(O, ch. 9)

Those who have fallen may remember the fall, even when they forget the height.

(EM, I-4)

It is not a mere verbal coincidence that original thinkers believe in Original Sin.

(ILN, "Original Sin and the Moderns," 9-1-28)

It holds, as against the only real alternative phi-losophies, those of the Buddhist or the Pessimist or the Promethean, that we have misused a good world, and not merely been entrapped into a bad one.

(TT, ch. 31)

[see also: Angels, Cross, Death, Evil, Ghosts, Incar-nation, Jesus, Mary, Mass, Miracles, Resurrection, Sac-ramentalism, Saints, Satan & Demons, Sin, Transub-stantiation, Trinitarianism]

Orthodoxy; Creeds

The word "orthodoxy" not only no longer means being right; it practically means being wrong.

(H, ch. 1)

A dogma is the only safeguard of democracy.

In the same way, the Prayer-Book is our only defence against clergymen.

(ILN, "Fancies and Facts," 9-22-06)

Creeds must disagree: it is the whole fun of the thing.

We may argue politely, we may argue humanely, we may argue with great mutual benefit; but, obviously, we must argue.

(ILN, "The History of Religions," 10-10-08)

Here it is enough to notice that if some small mistake were made in doctrine, huge blunders might be made in human happiness.

There never was anything so perilous or so exciting as orthodoxy.

It was the equilibrium of a man behind madly rushing horses, seeming to stoop this way and to sway that, yet in every attitude having the grace of statuary and the accuracy of arithmetic.

The orthodox Church never took the tame course or accepted the conventions; the orthodox Church was never respectable.

It is always simple to fall; there are an infinity of angles at which one falls, only one at which one stands.

(O, ch. 6)

There is only one thing that can never go past a certain point in its alliance with oppression—and that is orthodoxy.

(O, ch. 8)

A creed is a collective thing, and even its sins are sociable.

(WWW, I-3)

Many modern people, for example, imagine that the Athanasian Creed is full of vain repetitions; but that is because people are too lazy to listen to it, or not lucid enough to understand it.

(NJ, ch. 2)

I was maintaining that in practice the rationalist drifts into all sorts of superstitions and slaveries, which limit his thought far more than orthodoxy can limit the orthodox.

(ILN, "Mr. Archer's Defense of Darwinism," 12-8-23)

The Christian creed is above all things the philosophy of shapes and the enemy of shapelessness.

And that is why the Church is from the first a thing holding its own position and point of view, quite apart from the accidents and anarchies of its age.

(EM, II-4)

I pointed out to the people who say that creeds are crumbling that they do in fact crumble less than anything else; that certain abstract theological and theoretical definitions have outlasted all sorts of other things, but especially outlasted their enemies.

(ILN, "Some Complaints About Chesterton," 12-31-27)

When a hammer has hit the right nail on the head a hundred times, there comes a time when we think it was not altogether by accident.

(TT, ch. 8)

It was the intellectual value of the creed that preserved it through any revolution of aesthetic values, just as it preserves it still amid the wildest changes in aesthetic taste to-day.

(ILN, "The Truth of Mediaeval Times," 1-18-30)

I am proud of being fettered by antiquated dogmas and enslaved by dead creeds (as my journalistic friends repeat with so much pertinacity), for I know very well that it is the heretical creeds that are dead, and that it is only the reasonable dogma that lives long enough to be called antiquated.

I am not over-awed by a young gentleman saying that he cannot submit his intellect to dogma; because I doubt whether he has even used his intellect enough to define dogma.

(A, ch. 4)

I had begun to discover that, in all that welter of inconsistent and incompatible heresies, the one and only really unpardonable heresy was orthodoxy.

(A, ch. 7)

I have only found one creed that could not be satisfied with a truth, but only with the Truth, which is made of a million such truths and yet is one.

(A, ch. 16)

[see also: Authority (Religious), Catholicism & Catholics, Catholicity, Christianity, Church (Catholic), Conversion (Catholic), Development (Doctrinal), Dogma (Catholic), Gnosticism, Heresies, History (Church), Paganism (and Christianity), Papacy & Popes, Protestantism, Reformation (Catholic), Religion (Organized), Theologians, Tradition]

Pacifism

Surely there is something quite repulsively mean in saying that force must not be used against a conqueror from abroad, but force may be used against a poor, tired tramp who steals chickens.

The order and decency of our streets, the ease of exchange, and the fulfillment of contracts all repose ultimately upon the readiness of the community to fight for them, either against something without or against something within.

(ILN, "Boyhood and Militarism," 10-20-06)

The old Jew who says you must fight only for your tribe is inadequate; but the modern prig who says you must not ever fight for anything is substantially and specifically immoral.

(ILN, "Talking About Education," 1-26-07)

240

There must be *some* good in the idea of non-resistance, for so many good men seem to enjoy being Quakers.

(O, ch. 6)

Men who have no intention of abandoning their country's wealth, not to mention their own, men who rightly insist on comfort for their countrymen and not infrequently for themselves, still seem to have formed a strange idea that they can keep all these things in all conceivable circumstances, solely and entirely by refusing to defend them.

They seem to fancy they could bring the whole reign of violence and pride to an end, instantly and entirely, merely by doing nothing.

Does anybody believe that Hitler or Stalin or Mussolini would ruin all his plans because a Quaker did not propose to interfere with them?

(AS, ch. 3)

[see also: Morality, Vegetarianism, War, War and Christianity, World War I]

Paganism

The New Paganism is no longer new, and it never at any time bore the smallest resemblance to Paganism.

The term "pagan" is continually used in fiction and light literature as meaning a man without any religion, whereas a pagan was generally a man with about half a dozen.

Pagans are depicted as above all things inebriate and lawless, whereas they were above all things reasonable and respectable.

(H, ch. 12)

Paganism may be compared to that diffused light that glows in a landscape when the sun is behind a cloud.

So when the true centre of worship is for some reason invisible or vague, there has always remained for healthy humanity a sort of glow of gratitude or wonder or mystical fear, if it were only reflected from ordinary objects or natural forces or fundamental human traditions.

(AIS, ch. 29)

[see also: Gnosticism, Heresies, Orthodoxy, Paganism (and Christianity), Reincarnation, Religion (Comparative), Spiritualism, Superstition]

Paganism (and Christianity)

The primary fact about Christianity and Paganism is that one came after the other.

There is only one thing in the modern world that has been face to face with Paganism; there is only one thing in the modern world which in that sense knows anything about Paganism: and that is Christianity.

(H, ch. 12)

They regret the Pagan quality in the Christian festival; which is simply regretting that Christianity satisfied the previous cravings of mankind.

(ILN, "The Neglect of Christmas," 1-13-06)

We see in all the Christian ages this combination which is not a compromise, but rather a complexity made by two contrary enthusiasms; as when the Dark Ages copied out the pagan poems while denying the pagan legends; or when the popes of the Renascence imitated the Greek temples while denying the Greek gods.

(NJ, ch. 2)

Nobody ever disputed that humanity was human before it was Christian; and no Church manufactured the legs with which men walked or danced, either in a pilgrimage or a ballet.

What can really be maintained, so as to carry not a little conviction, is this: that where such a Church has existed it has preserved not only the processions but the dances; not only the cathedral but the carnival.

One of the chief claims of Christian civilisation is to have preserved things of pagan origin.

Even heathen things are Christian when they have been preserved by Christianity.

(SD, ch. 6)

Pagans were wiser than paganism; that is why the pagans became Christians.

(SF, ch. 2)

Neo-pagans have sometimes forgotten, when they set out to do everything that the old pagans did, that the final thing the old pagans did was to get christened.

(ILN, "The Return of the Pagan Gods," 3-20-26)

[see also: Authority (Religious), Catholicism & Catholics, Catholicity, Christianity, Church (Catholic), Conversion (Catholic), Development (Doctrinal), Dogma (Catholic), History (Church), Orthodoxy, Paganism, Papacy & Popes, Protestantism, Reformation (Catholic), Religion (Organized), Theologians, Tradition]

Pantheism

The pantheist cannot wonder, for he cannot praise God or praise anything as really distinct from himself.

(O, ch. 8)

All that is richest, deepest, and subtlest in the East is rooted in Pantheism; but all that is richest, deepest, and subtlest in us is concerned with denying passionately that Pantheism is either the highest or the purest religion.

(MM, ch. 23)

Now pantheism means that nothing is thus separated; that the divine essence is equally distributed at any given moment in all the atoms of the universe; and that he who would see it imaginatively must see it as a whole.

(SL, "The Soul in Every Legend" [1921])

Paganism is better than pantheism, for paganism is free to imagine divinities, while pantheism is forced to pretend, in a priggish way, that all things are equally divine.

(CCC, ch. 4)

I sincerely maintain that Nature-worship is more morally dangerous than the most vulgar man-worship of the cities; since it can easily be perverted into the worship of an impersonal mystery, carelessness, or cruelty.

(HAT, ch. 13)

The pantheist is always too near to the polytheist and the polytheist to the idolater; the idolater to the man offering human sacrifice.

(WEL, "A Century of Emancipation")

[see also: Creation, Nature, Poetry, Wonder]

Papacy and Popes

When Christ at a symbolic moment was establishing His great society, He chose for its corner-stone neither the brilliant Paul nor the mystic John, but a shuffler, a snob a coward—in a word, a man.

But this one thing, the historic Christian Church, was founded on a weak man, and for that reason it is indestructible.

For no chain is stronger than its weakest link.

(H, ch. 4)

Catholics, I need not say, are about as likely to call the Pope God as to call a grasshopper the Pope.

I fancy it would be quite feasible to describe in accurate but abstract terms the general idea of an office or obligation, which would exactly correspond to the position of the Papacy in history, and which would be accepted on ethical and social ground by numbers of Protestants and free-thinkers; until they discovered with a reaction of rage and astonishment that they had been entrapped into accepting the international arbitration of the Pope.

(TT, ch. 34)

[see also: Authority (Religious), Catholicism & Catholics, Catholicity, Christianity, Church (Catholic), Conversion (Catholic), Development (Doctrinal), Dogma (Catholic), History (Church), Orthodoxy, Paganism (and Christianity), Protestantism, Reformation (Catholic), Religion (Organized), Theologians, Tradition]

Paradox (in Christianity)

The truth is that the tradition of Christianity (which is still the only coherent ethic of Europe) rests on two or three paradoxes or mysteries which can easily be impugned in argument and as easily justified in life.

(H, ch. 9)

The spirits of indignation and of charity took terrible and attractive forms, ranging from that monkish fierceness that scourged like a dog the first and greatest of the Plantagenets, to the sublime pity of St. Catherine, who, in the official shambles, kissed the bloody head of the criminal.

It is not a mixture like russet or purple; it is rather like a shot silk, for a shot silk is always at right angles, and is in the pattern of the cross.

Christianity was like a huge and ragged and romantic rock, which, though it sways on its pedestal at a touch, yet, because its exaggerated excrescences exactly balance each other, is enthroned there for a thousand years.

(O, ch. 6)

Any number of philosophies will repeat the platitudes of Christianity.

But it is the ancient Church that can again startle the world with the paradoxes of Christianity.

(SF, ch. 8)

[see also: Apologetics, Argument, Faith (and Reason), Ideas, Idealism, Philosophy, Reason & Logic, Science (and Religion), Theism, Truth]

Patriotism

And a patriotism that does not allow other people to be patriots is not a morality but an immorality.

(CCC, ch. 3)

But I do believe that patriotism rests on a psychological truth; a social sympathy with those of our own sort, whereby we see our own potential acts in them; and understand their history from within.

(CM, "Paying For Patriotism")

[see also: Nationalism, War]

Pessimism

Sorrow and pessimism are indeed, in a sense, opposite things, since sorrow is founded on the value of something, and pessimism upon the value of nothing.

(CD, ch. 2)

A Russian pessimist will denounce a policeman for killing a peasant, and then prove by the highest philosophical principles that the peasant ought to have killed himself.

(O, ch. 3)

The evil of the pessimist is, then, not that he chastises gods and men, but that he does not love what he chastises—he has not this primary and supernatural loyalty to things.

(O, ch. 5)

Insincere pessimism is a social accomplishment, rather agreeable than otherwise; and fortunately nearly all pessimism is insincere.

And it did for one wild moment cross my mind that, perhaps, those might not be the very best judges of the relation of religion to happiness who, by their own account, had neither one nor the other.

(O, ch. 6)

Just as a microbe might feel proud of spreading a pestilence, so the pessimistic mouse might exult to think that he was renewing in the cat the torture of conscious existence.

(O, ch. 7)

Pessimism is not in being tired of evil but in being tired of good.

(EM, I-8)

It is quite as certain as it ever was that life is a gift of God immensely valuable and immensely valued, and anybody can prove it by putting a pistol to the head of a pessimist.

(TT, ch. 6)

[see also: Despair, Fanatics, Madness, Moods, Optimism, Resignation, Suicide]

Philanthropy

Philanthropy, as far as I can see, is rapidly becoming the recognizable mark of a wicked man.

We have often sneered at the superstition and cowardice of the mediaeval barons who thought that giving lands to the Church would wipe out the memory of their raids or robberies; but modern capitalists seem to have exactly the same notion; with this not unimportant addition, that in the case of the capitalists the memory of the robberies is really wiped out.

(ILN, "Whitewashing the Philanthropists," 5-29-09)

[see also: Capitalism, Distributism, Guilds, Poor, Publicity, Simplicity, Socialism, Thrift, Wealth]

Philosophy

If he asks me why I introduce what he calls paradoxes into a philosophical problem, I answer, because all
philosophical problems tend to become paradoxical.

(H, ch. 16)

A new philosophy generally means in practice the
praise of some old vice.

(ILN, "Newspaper Snippets and the Truth," 1-6-06)

A cosmic philosophy is not constructed to fit a man; a
cosmic philosophy is constructed to fit a cosmos.

(JOB)

For philosophy is a democratic thing, depending
only on man's reason; while science is almost necessarily
oligarchical, since it depends on man's opportunities.

(ILN, "On Punishing the Rich," 8-22-08)

Why is it nowadays considered a horrible insult to
accuse a philosopher of holding his own philosophy?

It is, apparently, wrong to classify a man, even apart
from whether you condemn him.

(ILN, "Being True to Oneself," 8-14-09)

So we shouted at each other and shook the room;
because metaphysics is the only thoroughly emotional
thing.

(TRE, ch. 5)

We shall certainly make fools of ourselves; that is what is meant by philosophy.

(WWW, IV-3)

We must consider how we came to be doing what we do, and even saying what we say.

As it is, the very terms we use are either meaningless or something more than meaningless, inconsistent even with themselves.

(NJ, ch. 1)

Plato in some sense anticipated the Catholic realism, as attacked by the heretical nominalism, by insisting on the equally fundamental fact that ideas are realities; that ideas exist just as men exist.

Aristotle anticipated more fully the sacramental sanity that was to combine the body and the soul of things; for he considered the nature of men as well as the nature of morals, and looked to the eyes as well as to the light.

(EM, I-6)

That means that a man who refuses to have his own philosophy will not even have the advantages of a brute beast, and be left to his own instincts.

Men have always one of two things: either a complete and conscious philosophy or the unconscious acceptance of the broken bits of some incomplete and shattered and often discredited philosophy.

Philosophy is merely thought that has been thought out.

But what is actually the matter with the modern man is that he does not know even his own philosophy; but only his own phraseology.

(CM, "The Revival of Philosophy – Why?")

[see also: Apologetics, Argument, Faith (and Reason), Greeks, Ideas, Idealism, Paradox (in Christianity), Reason & Logic, Science, Science (and Religion), Theism, Truth]

Physics, Modern

But to-day it is very hard for a scientific man to say where the supernatural ends or the natural begins, or what name should be given to either.

It is no longer a question of defining or denying a simple central power, but of balancing the brain in a bewilderment of new powers which seem to overlap and might even conflict.

Nature herself has become unnatural.

It is quite self-evident that scientific men are at war with wilder and more unfathomable fancies than the facts of the age of Huxley.

It is true that the pattern of the paper has changed, for the very pattern of the world has changed; we are told that it is not made of atoms like the dots but of electrons like the spirals.

But the vital point is, not that science deals with what we do not know, but that science is destroying what we thought we did know.

Nearly all the latest discoveries have been destructive, not of the old dogmas of religion, but rather of the recent dogmas of science.

The atom was smashed to atoms.

And dancing to the tune of Professor Einstein, even the law of gravity is behaving with lamentable levity.

They were themselves dealing now with a number of unknown quantities; what is the power of mind over matter; when is matter an illusion of mind; what is identity, what is individuality, is there a limit to logic in the last extremes of mathematics?

(NJ, ch. 8)

The science of Einstein might rather be called following our unreason as far as it will go, seeing whether the brain will crack under the conception that space is curved, or that parallel straight lines always meet.

(NJ, ch. 9)

At this moment the material hypotheses are mystical ideas.

They are incredibly and unthinkably mystical; they are much too mystical to be called material.

The truth is that, according to the latest science, it is impossible for Physics to go any further without fading into Metaphysics.

The Electron is rather a mathematical idea than a material object; it is a principle of energy acting, in the normal sense, upon nothing, or nothing that can be expressed in terms of anything.

(ILN, "Religion and the New Science," 4-12-30)

[see also: Creation, Darwinism, Life (Origin of), Materialism, Medicine (Alternative), Philosophy, Science, Science (and Religion)]

Poetry

One of the best tests in the world of what a poet really means is his metre.

(TWE, ch. 3)

The sense that everything is poetical is a thing solid and absolute; it is not a mere matter of phraseology or persuasion.

(H, ch. 3)

Some good people are almost poets and some bad poets are almost professors.

Poets are those who share these popular sentiments, but can so express them that they prove themselves the strange and delicate things that they really are.

Poets draw out the shy refinement of the rabble.

The Poets carry the popular sentiments to a keener and more splendid pitch; but let it always be remembered that it is the popular sentiments that they are carrying.

No man ever wrote any good poetry to show that childhood was shocking, or that twilight was gay and farcical, or that a man was contemptible because he had crossed his single sword with three.

The Poets are those who rise above the people by understanding them.

Of course, most of the Poets wrote in prose—Rabelais, for instance, and Dickens.

The Poets who embrace and admire the people are often pelted with stones and crucified.

I mean such people as, having culture and imagination, use them to understand and share the feelings of their fellows; as against those who use them to rise to what they call a higher plane.

Crudely, the poet differs from the mob by his sensibility; the professor differs from the mob by his insensibility.

(AD, ch. 23)

It may be hinted that when poets put away childish things they will put away poetry.

(FVF, ch. 1)

I have always had the fancy that if a man were really free, he would talk in rhythm and even in rhyme.

(FVF, ch. 8)

But for some reason I have never heard explained, it is only the minority of unpoetical people who are allowed to write critical studies of these popular poems.

(EM, I-5)

But poetry simply consists of connotation.

It is all in the atmosphere created by the terms, as an incantation calls up spirits.

It is almost more made up of the echoes of words than the words themselves.

(ILN, "Catchwords and Claptrap," 1-8-27)

And, as I am not now writing the most modern poetry, I may be allowed to be clear.

(AIS, ch. 17)

The ideal condition is that the poet should put his meaning more and more into the language of the people, and that the people should enjoy more and more of the meaning of the poet.

(AIS, ch. 18)

And the dreadful disreputable doubt, which stirs in my own sceptical mind, is a doubt about whether it would really matter much what style a poet chose to write in, in any period, so long as he wrote Good Poetry.

I am questioning this incessantly repeated suggestion, that certain particular images or cadences or conceptions have become impossible to any literary man, because he has the misfortune to live at this particular moment by the clock.

(AS, ch. 12)

[see also: Art and Artists, Children, Fairy Tales, Fiction, Imagination, Language, Life, Mysticism, Mythology, Novels, Romanticism, Stories, Wonder, Writers]

Politicians

It is too much the custom in politics to describe a political opponent as utterly inhumane, as utterly careless of his country, as utterly cynical, which no man ever was since the beginning of the world.

(TWE, ch. 4)

The statesman often has months to make up his mind; he has all the advantages of a liberal education and converse with men of the world; and still he uses the cant phrases, or rather, he lets the cant phrases use him.

(ILN, "The Crimes of Journalism," 10-13-06)

Out of Parliament the politician persuades the people that he really wants what they want.

Inside Parliament the politician persuades the people that they really want what he wants.

But what is really intolerable, what is really atrocious, is certainly this – that politicians should venture not merely to deceive the people about the things that the people do care about, but should insolently attempt to oppress the people in the things that the people do care about.

The greatest miracle is the fact that politicians are tolerated.

(ILN, "Politicians and Miracles," 12-22-06)

I am afraid it must be frankly confessed that representatives do not represent; that politicians do not resemble the respectable working-classes in anything – except their highly respectable objection to work.

(ILN, "Politicians and Their Constitutions," 11-20-09)

We are bewildered on every side by politicians who are in favor of secular education, but think it hopeless to work for it; who desire total prohibition, but are certain they should not demand it; who regret compulsory education, but resignedly continue it; or who want peasant proprietorship and therefore vote for something else.

(WWW, I-2)

I would rather a boy learnt in the roughest school the courage to hit a politician, or gained in the hardest school the learning to refute him—rather than that he should gain in the most enlightened school the cunning to copy him.

(ILN, "The Incomplete Vision of Modernity," 8-31-12)

The really practical statesman does not fit himself to existing conditions, he denounces the conditions as unfit.
(MM, ch. 4)

I doubt whether the best men ever would devote themselves to politics.

And as for the fanatical conflict in party politics, I wish there was more of it.
(MM, ch. 7)

Missing the point is a very fine art; and has been carried to something like perfection by politicians and Pressmen to-day.
(UTO, "The Art of Missing the Point")

But as an incapacity for any kind of thought is now regarded as statesmanship, there is nothing so very novel about such slovenly drafting.
(EUG, I-2)

I believe less in the State because I know more of the statesmen.
(CCC, ch. 5)

But being an English politician he is simply a poet.
(HAT, ch. 11)

Politicians did not represent the populace, even the most noisy and vulgar of the populace.

Politicians did not deserve the dignified name of demagogues.

They deserved no name except perhaps the name of
bagmen; they were travelling for private firms.
                              (WEL, "The Case of Spain")

[see also: Anarchy, Aristocracy, Caesaropapism,
Conservatism, Democracy, Government, Law, Liberalism (Political), Monarchy, Nationalism, Nazism, Patriotism, Revolution, Socialism, Spain (Civil War), Tolerance,
Voting]

Poor, The

So again, the poor man is simply a person who
expends upon treating himself and his friends in public
houses about the same proportion of his income as richer
people spend on dinners or cabs; that is, a great deal more
than he ought.

A poor man, as it is weirdly ordained, is definable
as a man who has not got much money; to hear philanthropists talk about him one would think he was a
kangaroo.
                    (SL, "The Philosophy of Islands" [1903])

What is quite evident is that if a logical praise of the
poor man is pushed too far, and if a logical distress about
him is pushed too far, either will involve wreckage to the
central paradox of reform.

If the poor man is made too admirable he ceases to be
pitiable; if the poor man is made too pitiable he becomes
merely contemptible.

There is a school of smug optimists who will deny that he is a poor man.

There is a school of scientific pessimists who will deny that he is a man.

Now, the practical weakness of the vast mass of modern pity for the poor and the oppressed is precisely that it is merely pity; the pity is pitiful, but not respectful.

And all the despair about the poor, and the cold and repugnant pity for them, has been largely due to the vague sense that they have literally relapsed into the state of the lower animals.

Jesus Christ was destined to found a faith which made the rich poorer and the poor rich; but even when He was going to enrich them, He began with the phrase, "Blessed are the poor."

(CD, ch. 11)

But, as a matter of fact, the traditions of the poor are mostly simply the traditions of humanity, a thing which many of us have not seen for some time.

(WWW, IV-13)

Two of the dreariest things in the world, for instance, are the way in which the snobs among the rich talk about the poor; and the way in which the prigs who profess to have an economic cure for poverty themselves talk about the poor.

(AS, ch. 28)

[see also: Capitalism, Distributism, Guilds, Philanthropy, Publicity, Simplicity, Socialism, Thrift, Wealth]

Pragmatism

There has arisen in our time a most singular fancy: the fancy that when things go very wrong we need a practical man.

It would be far truer to say, that when things go very wrong we need an unpractical man.

When things will not work, you must have the thinker, the man who has some doctrine about why they work at all.

(WWW, I-2)

Reason was self-evident before Pragmatism.
(ILN, "On Modern Controversy," 8-14-26)

[see also: Agnosticism, Atheism, Determinism, Hedonism, Liberalism (Theological), Materialism, Modernism, Progress (Idea of), Rebellion, Secularism, Skepticism, Utopias]

Prejudice

There are two things, and two things only, for the human mind, a dogma and a prejudice.

Our age is, at its best, a poetical epoch, an age of prejudice.

A doctrine is a definite point; a prejudice is a direction.

A prejudice is a private thing, and even its tolerance is misanthropic.

(WWW, I-3)

[see also: Bigotry & Racism, Broadmindedness, Conspiratorialism, Dogmatism, Openmindedness, Tolerance]

Pride

The philosopher of the ego sees everything, no doubt, from a high and rarified heaven; only he sees everything foreshortened or deformed.

(DEF, ch. 12)

It will not, I imagine, be disputed that the one black and inexcusable kind of pride is the pride of the man who has something to be proud of.

The instinct of the human soul perceives that a fool may be permitted to praise himself, but that a wise man ought to praise God.

A man who by genius can make masterpieces ought to know that he cannot make genius.

So it certainly does in practice come about that the more right a man has to vanity the less the sensible human race permits him to be vain.

(AWD, "The True Vanity of Vanities" [1904])

Pride is a weakness in the character; it dries up laughter, it dries up wonder, it dries up chivalry and energy.

Vanity is social—it is almost a kind of comradeship; pride is solitary and uncivilized.

Vanity is active; it desires the applause of infinite multitudes; pride is passive, desiring only the applause of one person, which it already has.

Vanity is humorous, and can enjoy the joke even of itself; pride is dull, and cannot even smile.

(H, ch. 9)

And every generous person will equally agree that the one kind of pride which is wholly damnable is the pride of the man who has something to be proud of.

The pride which, proportionally speaking, does not hurt the character, is the pride in things which reflect no credit on the person at all.

The man who is proud of what is really creditable to him is the Pharisee, the man whom Christ Himself could not forbear to strike.

(H, ch. 12)

One "settles down" into a sort of selfish seriousness; but one has to rise to a gay self-forgetfulness.

It is really a natural trend or lapse into taking one's self gravely, because it is the easiest thing to do.

(O, ch. 7)

Priests

Why should man who wanted to be wicked encumber himself with special and elaborate promises to be good?

Why should a man encumber himself with vows that nobody could expect him to take and he did not himself expect to keep?

Would any man make himself poor in order that he might become avaricious; or take a vow of chastity frightfully difficult to keep in order to get into a little more trouble when he did not keep it?

(CCC, ch. 2)

Prigs

Snobs say they have the right kind of hat; prigs say they have the right kind of head.

(ILN, "The Nature of Human Conscience," 12-12-08)

The definition of a prig, I suppose, is this: one who has pride in the possession of his brain rather than joy in the use of it.

And the difference is exactly this, that a very small brain is enough to be proud of, even when it is not big enough either to enjoy with recklessness or to use with effect.

And there is this further fact, that people with large intellects know the limits of intellect; while to people of small intellects, intellect seems unlimited and therefore divine.

(ILN, "Modern Jargon," 6-12-09)

[see also: Common Sense, Critics, Experts, Gentlemen, "Higher Culture," Humanitarianism, Intelligentsia, Man (Common)]

Private Judgment (Protestant Outlook)

Milton is possessed with what is, I suppose, the first and finest idea of Protestantism – the idea of the individual soul actually testing and tasting all the truth there is, and calling that truth which it has not tested or tasted truth of a less valuable and vivid kind.

(ILN, "Catholic Shakespeare and Protestant Milton," 6-8-07)

What we want is a religion that is right where we are wrong.

Only, as I have said, when I do find it out, I find it rather impressive; for it is not the religion that was right when I was right, but the religion that was right when I was wrong.

(CCC, ch. 5)

It is the simple fact that the moment men began to contradict the Church with their own private judgment, everything they did was incredibly ill-judged; that those who broke away from the Church's basis almost immediately broke down on their own basis; that those who tried to stand apart from Authority could not in fact stand at all.

(WEL, "The Religion of Fossils")

[see also: Anti-Catholicism, Calvinism, Protestant-ism, Puritanism, Reformation (English), Reformation (Protestant), *Sola Scriptura*]

Progress, Idea of

Nobody has any business to use the word "progress" unless he has a definite creed and a cast-iron code of morals.

Nobody can be progressive without being doctrinal; I might almost say that nobody can be progressive without being infallible—at any rate, without believing in some infallibility.

For progress by its very name indicates a direction; and the moment we are in the least doubtful about the direction, we become in the same degree doubtful about the progress.

(H, ch. 2)

They never fell into the habit of the idle revolution-ists of supposing that the past was bad because the future was good, which amounted to asserting that because humanity had never made anything but mistakes it was now quite certain to be right.

(VT, ch. 20)

An imbecile habit has arisen in modern controversy of saying that such and such a creed can be held in one age but cannot be held in another.

What a man can believe depends upon his philosophy, not upon the clock or the century.

(O, ch. 5)

Some fall back simply on the clock: they talk as if mere passage through time brought some superiority; so that even a man of the first mental calibre carelessly uses the phrase that human morality is never up to date.

The only intelligible sense that progress or advance can have among men, is that we have a definite vision, and that we wish to make the whole world like that vision.

But it is clear that no political activity can be encouraged by saying that progress is natural and inevitable; that is not a reason for being active, but rather a reason for being lazy.

(O, ch. 7)

The Future is non-existent; therefore the Future is dead.

The Past is existent, and therefore the Past is alive.
(ILN, "Worship of the Future," 12-18-09)

The truth is that all feeble spirits naturally live in the future, because it is featureless; it is a soft job; you can make it what you like.

The next age is blank, and I can paint it freely with my favourite colour.

It requires real courage to face the past, because the past is full of facts which cannot be got over; of men certainly wiser than we and of things done which we could not do.

(GBS, "The Philosopher")

I have never been able to make out what the Progressive Movement is, except that it is rather like the policeman who always tells people to "move on," without telling them where to go.

(ILN, "Christmas and the Progressive Movement," 1-1-10)

The people who say they are pursuing progress are really only obeying precedent.

By this system a Conservative means a man who must stop where his grandfather stopped; and a Progressive means a man who may only walk where his grandfather told him to.

(ILN, "The Fallacy of Precedent and Progress," 5-7-10)

The modern man no longer presents the memoirs of his great grandfather; but is engaged in writing a detailed and authoritative biography of his great-grandson.

The future is a blank wall on which every man can write his own name as large as he likes; the past I find already covered with illegible scribbles, such as Plato, Isaiah, Shakespeare, Michael Angelo, Napoleon.

I can make the future as narrow as myself; the past is obliged to be as broad and turbulent as humanity.

They look forward with enthusiasm, because they are afraid to look back.

I say decisively that nothing is so marked in modern writing as the prediction of such ideals in the future combined with the ignoring of them in the past.

(WWW, I-4)

Those who tell us, with a monotonous metaphor, that we cannot put the clock back, seem to be curiously unconscious of the fact that their own clock has stopped.

(SD, ch. 8)

The very notion of always talking in terms of tomorrow is a passing taste that will soon be a thing of yesterday.

Those who are concerned for the coming thing are really rather concerned for the vanishing thing, concerned to catch a fashion before it vanishes.

Most of the artistic experiments and social prophecies which appeal to the next age, are in fact stamped with all the special marks and limitations of this age.

(AWD, "The Unknown Warrior" [1920])

If I were called upon to consider the subject I should try to consider the subject itself, and not these rhetorical recriminations about whether a thing is old or new.

This talk about progress and retrogression is to be resisted, not because progress is never to be achieved, not because retrogression is never to be deplored, but because the talk about these two abstractions always hampers the discussion of the intrinsic truth involved.

(ILN, "The Old-Fashioned and the New-Fangled,"
7-28-23)

It is impudent to question Progress, but not impudent to question Providence.

(ILN, "Modern Doubts and Questioning," 2-13-26)

The later French Pantheists called Voltaire a barbarian, exactly as Voltaire had called Shakespeare a barbarian.

(ILN, "The Gloom of the Escorial," 6-5-26)

Nobody seems to notice that the young are always proved wrong in their condemnation of the old.

(ILN, "The Narrowness of the New Art," 8-18-28)

I was very tolerant of the idea of being behind the times, having had long opportunities of studying the perfectly ghastly people who were abreast of the times; or the still more pestilent people who were in advance of the times.

(TT, ch. 11)

The recent decay of thought may be due to the general notion of merely going forward; whereas all thinking is thinking backwards.

A dead thing, working like a rod or running on a rail, can only go forward; it is limited to one movement and is therefore Progressive.

(ILN, "The Creeds and the Modernist," 5-17-30)

I do not know a single example in history of a new step or stage, of any real importance, that did not refer back to an earlier stage or style.

(ILN, "On Progress, and Overthrowing Progress," 12-13-30)

For though today is always today and the moment is always modern, we are the only men in all history who fell back upon bragging about the mere fact that today is not yesterday.

(AIS, ch. 3)

[see also: Agnosticism, Atheism, Authority, Darwinism, Determinism, Hedonism, Liberalism (Theological), Materialism, Modernism, Physics (Modern), Pragmatism, Rebellion, Science, Secularism, Skepticism, Utopias]

Prophets

He suffers from an unrequited attachment to things in general.

(DEF, Introduction)

But clearly it is quite true that whenever we go to hear a prophet or teacher we may or may not expect wit, we may or may not expect eloquence, but we do expect what we do not expect.

(H, ch. 16)

[see also: Bible, "Higher Criticism," Revelation (Book of), *Sola Scriptura*]

Protestantism

Protestants are Catholics gone wrong; that is what is really meant by saying they are Christians.

(CCC, ch. 4)

[see also: Anti-Catholicism, Calvinism, Private Judgment, Puritanism, Reformation (English), Reformation (Protestant), *Sola Scriptura*]

Publicity; Advertising

It is impossible to put in the cheery terms of "publicity" either the truth about how bad things are, or the truth about how hard it will be to cure them.

(OS, ch. 3)

It means merely flattering private enterprises in the interests of private persons.

It means paying compliments in public, but not offering criticisms in public.

Publicity must be praise and praise must to some extent be euphemism.

(ILN, "The Friends of Frankness, and Euphemism," 6-30-28)

[see also: Capitalism, Distributism, Guilds, Philanthropy, Poor, Simplicity, Socialism, Thrift, Wealth]

Puritanism

It has gradually decayed in England and Scotland, not because of the advance of modern thought (which means nothing), but because of the slow revival of the mediaeval energy and character in the two peoples.

The English were always hearty and humane, and they have made up their minds to be hearty and humane in spite of the Puritans.

(GBS, "The Puritan")

It was an outbreak of the barbaric mysticism of the North against the classical clarity of the South.

(ILN, "Bigotry of the Rationalists," 4-30-10)

Dickens quite obviously existed to champion everything that the Puritans existed to destroy; when Mr Scrooge is converted to Christmas, the Puritan would have thought that Scrooge was relapsing and not repenting.

(AWD, "The Return of Pageantry" [1911])

We always said that England would be damaged by Puritanism, but we never knew that the worst damage would be done by the inevitable failure of Puritanism, which broke down and let in a flood of Paganism.

(ILN, "My Silver Anniversary With the ILN," 9-27-30)

I am very fond of spiced beef and all the spices; I always dread that the Puritan reformers will suddenly forbid mustard and pepper as they did malt and hops;

on the absurd ground that salt and mustard are as unnec-
essary as music.

(SL, "The Spice of Life" [1936])

[see also: Anti-Catholicism, Calvinism, Private
Judgment, Protestantism, Reformation (English), Reformation (Protestant)]

Reason and Logic

It is an act of faith to assert that our thoughts have any relation to reality at all.

The main point here, however, is that this idea of a fundamental alteration in the standard is one of the things that make thought about the past or future simply impossible.

(O, ch. 3)

There is no reason why a man with strong reasoning power should not have strong affections; and it is my experience, if anything, that the man who can argue clearly in the abstract generally does have a generosity of blood and instincts.

(SL, "Charlotte Bronte as a Romantic" [1917])

Not one man in ten throughout the whole nineteenth- and twentieth-century civilization has had the very vaguest notion that he needed to have any first principles.

But to complain merely of a logician setting out with something unproved is itself a disastrous lapse of logic.

People not only do not understand the argument called the *reductio ad absurdum*, but they actually think the argument absurd.
(ILN, "The Need For a Starting-Point," 11-21-25)

What does seem to me to have slackened or weakened is not so much the connection between conscience and conduct clearly approved by conscience, as the connection between any two ideas that could enable anybody to see anything clearly at all.

The difficulty is not so much to get people to follow a commandment as to get them even to follow an argument.
(ILN, "Being Bored With Ideas," 3-13-26)

I believe a new and enormous number of people now have no opinions at all.

But, though what is called their opinion is at best a tradition, still it is the tradition of no opinion.

Not only have men lost their opinions, but many of them seem to have lost the power of forming opinions.

They no more employ first principles than flint arrows, and regard the first proposition of Euclid as a Paleolithic drawing on a rock.
(ILN, "The Blank State of the Modern Mind," 4-3-26)

We shall soon be in a world in which a man may be howled down for saying that two and two make four, in which furious party cries will be raised against anybody who says that cows have horns, in which people will persecute the heresy of calling a triangle a three-sided figure, and hang a man for maddening a mob with the news that grass is green.

(ILN, "On Modern Controversy," 8-14-26)

There seems to be a sort of public holiday from logic just now, a Saturnalia of escape from the slavery of the syllogism.

What is new in this matter is not so much unreason as the fact of unreason not being recognised as unreasonable

(ILN, "Journalistic Logic Chopping," 10-22-27)

What we call the intellectual world is divided into two types of people—those who worship the intellect and those who use it.

(TT, ch. 6)

Slow thinking is accompanied with incessant excitement; but quick thinking is more quiet.

(ILN, "On Arguing in a Straight Line," 6-21-30)

They begin to see that, as the eighteenth century thought itself the age of reason, and the nineteenth century thought itself the age of common sense, the twentieth century cannot as yet even manage to think itself anything but the age of uncommon nonsense.

(STA, ch. 1)

Well aware of how offensive I make myself, and with what loathing I may well be regarded, in this sentimental age which pretends to be cynical, and in this poetical nation which pretends to be practical, I shall nevertheless continue to practise in public a very repulsive trick or habit—the habit of drawing distinctions; or distinguishing between things that are quite different, even when they are assumed to be the same.

For in truth I believe that the only way to say anything definite is to define it, and all definition is by limitation and exclusion; and that the only way to say something distinct is to say something distinguishable; and distinguishable from everything else.

(AS, ch. 3)

I have generally attempted, in a modest way, to have reasons for my opinions; and I have never been able to see why the opinions should change until the reasons change.

(A, ch. 11)

[see also: Apologetics, Argument, Faith (and Reason), Greeks, Ideas, Idealism, Paradox (in Christianity), Philosophy, Science, Science (and Religion), Theism, Truth]

Rebellion

There is not really any courage at all in attacking hoary or antiquated things, any more than in offering to fight one's grandmother.

(WWW, I-4)

The innovator boasts that he is free to show how time has justified the rebel; but I hold myself equally free to speculate on how a little more time may justify the rebuke of the rebel.

(ILN, "A Defense of the Neo-Classical Poets," 3-27-26)

It is an eternal truth that the fathers stone the prophets and the sons build their sepulchres; often out of the same stones.

The curious thing is that, when the rebellion comes, it is generally a rebellion against rebels.

Those who were, in fact, doomed to dethronement in the future were generally the futurists of the past.

(ILN, "The Rebellion Against Yesterday's Rebels," 10-17-31)

[see also: Agnosticism, Atheism, Authority, Hedonism, Liberalism (Theological), Materialism, Modernism, Pragmatism, Progress (Idea of), Revolution, Secularism, Skepticism, Utopias]

Reformation, Catholic

We should be delighted also to have a new Reformation, of ourselves as well as of Protestants and other people; though it is only fair to say that Catholics did, within an incredibly short space of time, contrive to make something very like a new Reformation; which is commonly called the Counter-Reformation.

(TT, ch. 12)

[see also: Authority (Religious), Catholicism & Catholics, Catholicity, Christianity, Church (Catholic), Conversion (Catholic), Development (Doctrinal), Dogma (Catholic), History (Church), Orthodoxy, Paganism (and Christianity), Papacy & Popes, Protestantism, Religion (Organized), Theologians, Tradition]

Reformation, English

In each of the separate holes or quandaries in which the ordinary Englishman has been placed, he has been told that his situation is, for some particular reason, all for the best.

He woke up one fine morning and discovered that the public things, which for eight hundred years he had used at once as inns and sanctuaries, had all been suddenly and savagely abolished, to increase the private wealth of about six or seven men.

But it was not merely the army that kept him quiet. He was kept quiet by the sages as well as the soldiers; the six or seven men who took away the inns of the poor told him that they were not doing it for themselves, but for the religion of the future, the great dawn of Protestantism and truth.

(WWW, I-10)

Just as we hear of the admiral being shot but have never heard of his being born, so we all heard a great deal about the dissolution of the monasteries, but we heard next to nothing about the creation of the monasteries.

(SF, ch. 2)

Everybody knew even then that Queen Elizabeth was bloody, if pursuing people with execution and persecution and torture makes a person bloody; and that was the only reason for saying it of Mary.

Everybody knew even then that Mary was good, if certain real virtues and responsibilities make a person good; a great deal more indubitably good than Elizabeth.

(WC, ch. 5)

Or again, it is outrageously misleading to suggest that the Catholic victims of Tudor and other tyranny were justly executed as traitors and not as martyrs to a religion.

But when, in point of plain fact, a man can be hanged, drawn and quartered merely for saying Mass, or sometimes for helping somebody who has said Mass, it is simply raving nonsense to say that a religion is not being persecuted.

(TT, ch. 12)

We must remember that even to talk of the corruption of the monasteries is a compliment to the monasteries.

We can entirely absolve the Cranmers and the Cromwells of any restless desire to raise the proletariat.

The distinguishing mark of the Reformers was a profound respect for the powers that be, but an even profounder respect for the wealth that was to be; and a really unfathomable reverence for the wealth that was to be their own.

The Reformation, especially in England, was above all the abandonment of the attempt to rule the world by ideals, or even by ideas.

(TT, ch. 16)

Perhaps the most successful were those who really had no ideas to offer at all; like the founders of the Anglican Church.

(WEL, "The Religion of Fossils")

[see also: Anti-Catholicism, Aristocracy, Caesaropapism, Calvinism, Church (Catholic), Divorce, Orthodoxy, Private Judgment, Monarchy, Poor, Protestantism, Puritanism, Rebellion, Reformation (Protestant), Revolution, Tolerance, Tradition, Wealth]

Reformation, Protestant

It is common ground to Catholics and Protestants of intelligence that evils preceded and produced the schism; and that evils were produced by it and have pursued it down to our own day.

(NJ, ch. 12)

For instance, it was an abominable abuse that the corruption of the monasteries sometimes permitted a rich noble to play the patron and even play at being the Abbot, or draw on the revenues supposed to belong to a brotherhood of poverty and charity.

But all that the Reformation did was to allow the same rich noble to take over *all* the revenue, to seize the whole

house and turn it into a palace or a pig-sty, and utterly
stamp out the last legend of the poor brotherhood.

The worst things in worldly Catholicism were made
worse by Protestantism.

(TT, ch. 8)

But if I were to say, with Mr. Belloc, that Protestantism was the shipwreck of Christendom, I should regard it
as an ordinary historical statement, like saying that the
American War of Independence was a split in the British
Empire.

And that is that Robinson Crusoe has, ever since, been
continually going back to get things from the wreck.

(TT, ch. 32)

They waged an insane war against everything in the
old faith that is most normal and sympathetic to human
nature; such as prayers for the dead or the gracious image
of a Mother of Men.

(WEL, "The Religion of Fossils")

[see also: Anti-Catholicism, Aristocracy, Caesaropapism, Calvinism, Church (Catholic), Orthodoxy, Private
Judgment, Monarchy, Poor, Protestantism, Puritanism,
Rebellion, Reformation (English), Revolution, *Sola Scriptura*, Tolerance, Tradition, Wealth]

Reincarnation

It is no more transcendental for a man to remember what he did in Babylon before he was born than to

remember what he did in Brixton before he had a knock on the head.

(EM, I-6)

[see also: Gnosticism, Heresies, Orthodoxy, Paganism, Religion (Comparative), Spiritualism, Superstition]

Relics

But why a man should accept a Creator who was a carpenter, and then worry about holy water, why he should accept a local Protestant tradition that God was born in some particular place mentioned in the Bible, merely because the Bible had been left lying about in England, and then say it is incredible that a blessing should linger on the bones of a saint, why he should accept the first and most stupendous part of the story of Heaven on Earth, and then furiously deny a few small but obvious deductions from it—that is a thing I do not understand; I never could understand; I have come to the conclusion that I shall never understand.

(TT, ch. 21)

[see also: Asceticism, Confession, Faith, Incense, Martyrdom, Mysticism, Robes, Sabbath, Saints, Temptation]

Religion, Comparative; Ecumenism

To say that I must not deny my opponent's faith is to say I must not discuss it; I may not say that Buddhism is false, and that is all I want to say about Buddhism.

It is absurd to have a discussion on Comparative Religions if you don't compare them.
                    (ILN, "The History of Religions," 10-10-08)

This is the intellectual abyss between Buddhism and Christianity; that for the Buddhist or Theosophist personality is the fall of man, for the Christian it is the purpose of God, the whole point of his cosmic idea.
                                                            (O, ch. 8)

We do not (at least I do not) respect any sect, church, or group because of its sincerity.

In other words, an honest man must always respect other religions, because they contain parts of his religion – that is, of his largest vision of truth.

I will respect Confucians for reverencing the aged, because my religion also includes reverence for the aged.

But I will not admire Chinese tortures because they are performed with ardour; nor enjoy Hindoo pessimism because it is sincere, and therefore hopeless, pessimism; nor respect the Turk for despising women merely because he despises them very heartily.
             (ILN, "Respecting Other Peoples' Opinions," 10-29-10)

And my sympathies, when I go beyond the things I myself believe, are with all the poor Jews who do believe in Judaism and all the Mahometans who do believe in Mahometanism, not to mention so obscure a crowd as the Christians who do believe in Christianity.

I feel I have more morally and even intellectually in common with these people, and even the religions of these people, than with the supercilious negations that make up the most part of what is called enlightenment.

(NJ, ch. 7)

So the future may suffer not from the loss but the multiplicity of faith; and its fate be far more like the cloudy and mythological war in the desert than like the dry radiance of theism or monism.

(NJ, ch. 8)

It is rather ridiculous to ask a man just about to be boiled in a pot and eaten, at a purely religious feast, why he does not regard all religions as equally friendly and fraternal.

(EM, II-5)

We have practically come to a condition in which Christianity is the only religion which Christians do not study.

(ILN, "Where *Are* the Dead?," 7-7-28)

[see also: Jews and Judaism]

Religion, Organized

I have never been able to understand why men of science, or men of any sort, should have such a special affection for Disorganised Religion.

They would hardly utter cries of hope and joy over the prospect of Disorganised Biology or Disorganised Botany.

They would hardly wish to see the whole universe of astronomy disorganised, with no relations, no records, no responsibilities for the fulfillment of this or that function, no reliance on the regularity of this or that law.

The truth is that, in supernatural things as in natural things, there is in that sense an increase of organization with the increase of life.

In short, all this modern cant against organised religion is a highly modern result of disorganised reason.
                    (ILN, "Religion and the New Science," 4-12-30)

[see also: Authority (Religious), Catholicism & Catholics, Catholicity, Christianity, Church (Catholic), Conversion (Catholic), Development (Doctrinal), Dogma (Catholic), History (Church), Orthodoxy, Paganism (and Christianity), Papacy & Popes, Protestantism, Reformation (Catholic), Theologians, Tradition]

Renaissance, The

They paraded before the world a wild hypothetical pageant of what old Greece and Rome would have been if they had not been pagan.

To copy the old body in any case is amazing; to copy the old body, and also put in a new soul, is amazing beyond praise, beyond question, and certainly beyond quibbling.

Just as it would be a remarkable thing for men to become ancient Egyptians and yet remain modern Englishmen, so it was a remarkable thing when these men became ancient Greeks and yet remained mediaeval Christians.

When we consider that it really is a fact (though the first fool in the street will tell you so) that skepticism had begun to appear here and there even among priests and bishops, it is really singular, upon the balance, that it had not appeared more among painters and sculptors.

(ILN, "The Truth of Mediaeval Times," 1-18-30)

[see also: Architecture, Art and Artists, Cathedrals, Greeks, History, History (Church), Imagination, Middle Ages]

Resignation

For mere resignation has neither the gigantic levity of pleasure nor the superb intolerance of pain.

(O, ch. 7)

[see also: Despair, Fanatics, Madness, Moods, Optimism, Pessimism, Suicide]

Rest; Leisure

Lying in bed would be an altogether perfect and supreme experience if only one had a coloured pencil long enough to draw on the ceiling.

(TRE, ch. 10)

As for the third form of leisure, the most precious, the most consoling, the most pure and holy, the noble habit of doing nothing at all – that is being neglected in a degree which seems to me to threaten the degeneration of the whole race.

(ILN, "Leisure in Our Culture," 7-23-27)

But most normal persons are now taught to neglect far too much the sort of excitement which the mind itself manufactures out of unexciting things.

(ILN, "The Joy of Dullness," 5-3-30)

For my own part, I never can get enough Nothing to do.

I feel as if I had never had leisure to unpack a tenth part of the luggage of my life and thoughts.

(A, ch. 10)

Resurrection, The

There is the complete absence of any real attempt to disprove the Resurrection among the most furious enemies of those who were professing to prove it.

If Saul and Annas and the persecutors had the energy to stone and slay people for saying there was an empty tomb, why did they not have the energy to walk up a hill and point out the tomb that was not empty?

(ILN, "'Who Moved the Stone?,'" 4-5-30)

The historical case for the Resurrection is that everybody else, except the Apostles, had every possible motive to declare what they had done with the body, if anything had been done with it.

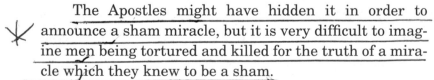

The Apostles might have hidden it in order to announce a sham miracle, but it is very difficult to imagine men being tortured and killed for the truth of a miracle which they knew to be a sham.

(AS, ch. 10)

[see also: Angels, Cross, Death, Evil, Ghosts, Incarnation, Jesus, Mary, Mass, Miracles, Original Sin, Sacramentalism, Saints, Satan & Demons, Sin, Transubstantiation, Trinitarianism]

Revelation (Book of)

And though St. John the Evangelist saw many strange monsters in his vision, he saw no creature so wild as one of his own commentators.

(O, ch. 2)

[see also: Bible, "Higher Criticism," Prophets, *Sola Scriptura*]

Revolution

All true revolutions are reversions to the natural and the normal.

A revolutionist who breaks with the past is a notion fit for an idiot.

(VT, ch. 20)

For all denunciation implies a moral doctrine of some kind; and the modern revolutionist doubts not only the institution he denounces, but the doctrine by which he denounces it.

By rebelling against everything he has lost his right to rebel against anything.

(O, ch. 3)

Man will sometimes act slowly upon new ideas; but he will only act swiftly upon old ideas.

To the orthodox there must always be a case for revolution; for in the hearts of men God has been put under the feet of Satan.

(O, ch. 7)

And there never has been in the history of the world a real revolution, brutally active and decisive, which was not preceded by unrest and new dogma in the reign of invisible things.

All revolutions began by being abstract.

(TRE, ch. 12)

It is chiefly interesting as evidence that the boldest plans for the future invoke the authority of the past; and that even a revolutionary seeks to satisfy himself that he is also a reactionary.

(EM, I-3)

[see also: Anarchy, Aristocracy, Caesaropapism, Conservatism, Democracy, Government, Law, Liberalism (Political), Monarchy, Nationalism, Nazism, Patriotism, Politicians, Socialism, Spain (Civil War), Tolerance, Voting]

Robes (Clerical)

The man who disliked vestments wore a pair of preposterous trousers.

(O, ch. 6)

They will complain of parsons dressing like parsons; as if we should be any more free if all the police who shadowed or collared us were plain clothes detectives.

(EM, Introduction)

[see also: Asceticism, Confession, Faith, Incense, Martyrdom, Mysticism, Priests, Relics, Sabbath, Temptation]

Romanticism

The whole modern theory arises from one fundamental mistake—the idea that romance is in some way a plaything with life, a figment, a conventionality, a thing upon the outside.

No genuine criticism of romance will ever arise until we have grasped the fact that romance lies not upon the outside of life but absolutely in the centre of it.

The centre of every man's existence is a dream.

Beyond all question, it marks a lack of literary instinct to be unable to simplify one's mind at the first signal of the advance of romance.

(TWE, ch. 12)

Romance is the deepest thing in life; romance is deeper even than reality.

To be born into this earth is to be born into uncongenial surroundings, hence to be born into a romance.

(H, ch. 14)

Now, all who are adherents of romanticism (as I am) have it for their first and fixed and central principle that romance is more serious than realism.

We say that romance is the grave and authoritative and responsible thing; the permanent religion of mankind.

Romance is life felt as somebody feels it.
(ILN, "Romantic and Realistic Drama," 3-17-06)

Nothing emerges more clearly from a study that is truly realistic, than the curious fact that romantic people were really romantic.
(NJ, ch. 11)

Mediaeval romance, which was a sort of pattern for modern romance, came from the vividness of visionary or spiritual experience leaving a sort of glamour or glory around all experience.
(AIS, ch. 32)

The habit of giving to romantic love this extravagant and exclusive importance in human life was itself an entirely modern and revolutionary thing, and dates from the romantic movement commonly traced to Rousseau, but I think much more truly to be traced to the influence of the German sentimentalists.
(AIS, ch. 35)

[see also: Adventure, Children, Chivalry, Fairy Tales, Ghosts, Heroes, Imagination, Middle Ages, Miracles, Mythology, Mysticism, Nature, Sentimentalism, Stories, Wonder]

Sabbath, The

I should have some sympathy with the Jewish Sabbath, if it were a Jewish Sabbath, and that for three reasons; first, that religion is an intrinsically sympathetic thing; second, that I cannot conceive any religion worth calling a religion without a fixed and material observance; and third, that the particular observance of sitting still and doing no work is one that suits my temperament down to the ground.

(TRE, ch. 25)

[see also: Asceticism, Confession, Faith, Incense, Martyrdom, Mysticism, Relics, Robes, Temptation]

Sacramentalism

Whenever men really believe that they can get to the spiritual, they always employ the material.

When the purpose is good, it is bread and wine; when the purpose is evil, it is eye of newt and toe of frog.

(ILN, "Superstition and Modern Justice," 10-6-06)

Faith-healing has existed from the beginning of the world; but faith-healing without a material act or sacrament – never.

(ILN, "Faith Healing and Medicine," 11-5-10)

[see also: Angels, Cross, Death, Evil, Ghosts, Incarnation, Jesus, Mary, Mass, Miracles, Original Sin, Resurrection, Saints, Satan & Demons, Sin, Transubstantiation, Trinitarianism]

Saints

The saints of Christianity are supposed to be like God, to be, as it were, little statuettes of Him.

(JOB)

There are saints indeed in my religion: but a saint only means a man who really knows he is a sinner.

(AD, ch. 37)

It would really require a saint to write about the life of a saint.

(SF, ch. 1)

Indeed that is why the saint is often a martyr; he is mistaken for a poison because he is an antidote.

Therefore it is the paradox of history that each generation is converted by the saint who contradicts it most.

(STA, ch. 1)

The holy man always conceals his holiness; that is the one invariable rule.

(STA, ch. 5)

[see also: Angels, Cross, Death, Evil, Ghosts, Incarnation, Jesus, Mary, Mass, Miracles, Original Sin, Resurrection, Sacramentalism, Satan & Demons, Sin, Transubstantiation, Trinitarianism]

Satan and Demons

What is wrong with the world is the devil, and what is right with it is God; the human race will travel for a few more million years in all sorts of muddle and reform, and when it perishes of the last cold or heat it will still be within the limits of that very simple definition.

(AWD, "What is Right With the World" [1910])

Dual personality is not so very far from diabolic possession.

Instead of Christian morals surviving in the form of humanitarian morals, Christian demonology has survived in the form of heathen demonology.

And what will be the next discovery in psychological science nobody can imagine; and we can only say that if it reveals demons and their name is Legion, we can hardly be much surprised now.

The more truly we can see life as a fairy-tale, the more clearly the tale resolves itself into war with the Dragon who is wasting fairyland.

I remember distinguished men among the liberal theologians, who found it more difficult to believe in one devil than in many.

They admitted in the New Testament an attestation to evil spirits, but not to a general enemy of mankind.

(NJ, ch. 9)

But Satan, though a traitor, was not an anarchist.

He claimed the crown of the cosmos; and had he prevailed, would have expected his rebel angels to give up rebelling.

(EUG, I-3)

Believing that there are spirits, I am bound in mere reason to suppose that there are probably evil spirits; believing that there are evil spirits, I am bound in mere reason to suppose that some men grow evil by dealing with them.

All that is mere rationalism; the superstition (that is the unreasoning repugnance and terror) is in the person who admits there can be angels but denies there can be devils.

The superstition is in the person who admits there can be devils but denies there can be diabolists.

(EUG, I-6)

[see also: Angels, Cross, Death, Evil, Ghosts, Incarnation, Jesus, Mary, Mass, Miracles, Original Sin, Resurrection, Sacramentalism, Saints, Sin, Spiritualism, Transubstantiation, Trinitarianism]

Satire; Ridicule

It may seem a singular observation to say that we are not generous enough to write great satire.

To write great satire, to attack a man so that he feels the attack and half acknowledges its justice, it is necessary to have a certain intellectual magnanimity which realises the merits of the opponent as well as his defects.

This is, indeed, only another way of putting the simple truth that in order to attack an army we must know not only its weak points, but also its strong points.

England in the present season and spirit fails in satire for the same simple reason that it fails in war: it despises the enemy.

It is impossible to satirise a man without having a full account of his virtues.

We might be angry at the libel, but not at the satire; for a man is angry at a libel because it is false, but at a satire because it is true.

(TWE, ch. 4)

For in a world where everything is ridiculous, nothing can be ridiculed.

If life is really so formless that you cannot make head or tail of it, you cannot pull its tail.
(ILN, "On Unmoral Comedy," 12-10-27)

Parody does not consist merely of contrast; at its best it rather consists of a superficial contrast covering a substantial congruity.
(CM, "The Pantomime")

[see also: Fools, Hilarity, Humor, Wit]

Science, Scientists, and Popular Science

The telescope makes the world smaller; it is only the microscope that makes it larger.
(H, ch. 3)

Science means specialism, and specialism means oligarchy.
(H, ch. 16)

He is a sentimentalist in this essential sense, that he is soaked and swept away by mere associations.
(O, ch. 4)

The trouble with nearly all these scientific theorists is quite simple: it is that they have cultivated the art of learning while they have entirely neglected the art of thinking.
(ILN, "Miracles and Scientific Method," 4-17-09)

The only evil that science has ever attempted in our time has been that of dictating not only what should be known, but the spirit in which it should be regarded.

Science must not impose any philosophy, any more than the telephone must tell us what to say.

There is no objection to scientists splitting open the world like the uncle's watch; in order to look at the works of it so long as those scientists feel like children.
(ILN, "Science: Pro and Con," 10-9-09)

The extreme doctrine of Science for Science's Sake has proved just as impossible as Art for Art's Sake.
(ILN, "Evolution and Ethics," 9-10-27)

<u>They had no right to insist on men accepting the lat-est word of science as the last word of science.</u>

Yet they were also insistently boasting that science had not concluded and would never conclude.
(ILN, "The Bible and the Sceptics," 4-20-29)

Quackery is false science; it is everywhere apparent in cheap and popular science; and the chief mark of it is that men who begin by boasting that they have cast away all dogma go on to be incessantly, impudently, and quite irrationally dogmatic.
(ILN, "Quackery About the Family," 7-12-30)

[see also: Agnosticism, Atheism, Creation, Darwinism, Dogmatism, Life (Origin of), Materialism,

Science (and Religion)

The truths of religion are unprovable; the facts of science are unproved.

(ILN, "Faith Healing and Medicine," 11-5-10)

We in the West have "followed our reason as far as it would go," and our reason has led us to things that nearly all the rationalists would have thought wildly irrational.

(NJ, ch. 9)

The problem of Religion and Science is still presented in the narrow Victorian version of a quarrel between Darwin and Moses.

(ILN, "The Younger Pagans," 8-21-26)

But in the Victorian debates between Science and religion, about such a question as the Deluge, there was a double ignorance and an ambiguity on both sides.

(ILN, "The Bible and the Sceptics," 4-20-29)

The Electron, as now expounded, is much more of a mystery than the Trinity.

There were, indeed, venerable Victorians, of the agnostic sort, who would have been very much surprised to learn that science had not destroyed religion by A.D. 2030.

(ILN, "Religion and the New Science," 4-12-30)

It is amusing to think that even religious people may still be driven to abandon religion by a science which scientists have abandoned.

(ILN, "The Place of Mysticism," 5-24-30)

[see also: Apologetics, Argument, Creation, Darwinism, Faith (and Reason), Ideas, Idealism, Life (Origin of), Materialism, Paradox (in Christianity), Philosophy, Physics (Modern), Reason & Logic, Science, Theism, Truth]

Scotland (and Calvinism)

The Scotch were always romantic, and they have made up their minds to be romantic in spite of the Puritans.

England has become English again; Scotland has become Scottish again, in spite of the splendid incubus, the noble nightmare of Calvin.

(GBS, "The Puritan")

Even in Scotland, I believe, Calvinism has only been an episode.

(AWD, "The Return of Pageantry" [1911])

Of all the great nations of Christendom, the Scotch are by far the most romantic.

(MM, ch. 16)

Very early Scottish Protestantism, like very early English Protestantism, consisted chiefly of loot.

(OS, ch. 5)

And anybody who has noticed what the modern Scottish character is really like, knows that it does not by this time (thank heaven) bear the smallest resemblance to the sternness of John Knox.

(TT, ch. 32)

[see also: America, Ireland]

Secularism

The secularists have not wrecked divine things; but the secularists have wrecked secular things, if that is any comfort to them.

(O, ch. 8)

Nearly all newspaper correspondences now revolve around religion, which we were told about fifty years ago had finally disappeared.

(ILN, "Modern Doubts and Questioning," 2-13-26)

Never until the nineteenth century was it supposed that the Church or Temple was a sort of side-show that had nothing to do with the State.

(ILN, "The Guilt of the Churches," 7-26-30)

For the word "secular" does not-mean anything so sensible as "worldly."

To be secular simply means to be of the age; that is, of the age which is passing; of the age which, in their case, is already passed.

There is one adequate equivalent of the word "secular"; and it is the word "dated."

(WEL, "The Well and the Shallows")

What is totally intolerable is the idea that everybody must pretend, for the sake of peace and decorum, that moral inspiration only comes from secular things like Distributism, and cannot possibly come from spiritual things like Catholicism.

(WEL, "The Don and the Cavalier")

[see also: Agnosticism, Atheism, Authority, Darwinism, Determinism, Hedonism, Liberalism (Theological), Materialism, Modernism, Pragmatism, Progress (Idea of), Rebellion, Skepticism, Utopias]

Self, Love of

A man may be said loosely to love himself, but he can hardly fall in love with himself, or, if he does, it must be a monotonous courtship.

(O, ch. 8)

Sentimentalism

We shall never attain to a serious and complete school of criticism so long as the word 'sentimental' is regarded as a term of depreciation.

That 'passionate' should be a complimentary form and 'sentimental' a hostile one is as utterly unmeaning and ridiculous as it would be if 'blue' were complimentary and 'green' hostile.

True sentiment consists in taking the central emotions of life not as passion takes them, personally, but impersonally, with a certain light and open confession of them as things common to us all.

If sentimental literature is to be condemned it must emphatically not be because it is sentimental, it must be because it is not literature.

Sentimentality, which it is fashionable to call morbid, is of all things most natural and healthy; it is the very extravagance of youthful health.

(SL, "Sentimental Literature" [1901])

For it cannot be too often insisted upon that the way to avoid sentiment becoming too sentimental is to admit the existence of sentiment as a plain, unsentimental fact, a thing as solid and necessary as soap.

(ILN, "Fanaticism in the Suburbs," 10-21-05)

Every man is incurably sentimental; but, unfortunately, it is so often a false sentiment.

(H, ch. 18)

There are apparently some people so constituted that they are sickened by any sentiment concerned with certain simple and popular things, such as the love of mothers or the charm of children.

It is obvious that anti-sentimentalism is only a rather priggish and a rather snobbish form of sentimentalism.

(ILN, "On Sentimentalism," 8-20-27)

Sexuality

They have invented a phrase, a phrase that is a black and white contradiction in two words—'free-love'—as if a lover ever had been, or ever could be, free.

(DEF, ch. 2)

Mankind declares this with one deafening voice: that sex may be ecstatic so long as it is also restricted.

In other words, the creation of conditions for love, or even for flirting, is the first common-sense of Society.

(ILN, "The Wrong Books at Christmas," 1-9-09)

We all disapprove of prostitution; but we do not all approve of purity.

(WWW, I-1)

These catastrophic images are but faint parallels to the earthquake consequences that Nature has attached to sex; and it is perfectly plain at the beginning that a man cannot be a free lover; he is either a traitor or a tied man.

(WWW, I-7)

What had happened to the human imagination, as a whole, was that the whole world was coloured by dangerous and rapidly deteriorating passions; by natural passions becoming unnatural passions.

Thus the effect of treating sex as only one innocent natural thing was that every other innocent natural thing became soaked and sodden with sex.

For sex cannot be admitted to a mere equality among elementary emotions or experiences like eating and sleeping.

The moment sex ceases to be a servant it becomes a tyrant.

There is something dangerous and disproportionate in its place in human nature, for whatever reason; and it does really need a special purification and dedication.

The modern talk about sex being free like any other sense, about the body being beautiful like any tree or flower, is either a description of the Garden of Eden or a piece of thoroughly bad psychology, of which the world grew weary two thousand years ago.

(SF, ch. 2)

And it seems to me exceedingly funny that, just when the rising generation boasts of not being sentimental, when it talks of being very scientific and sociological – at that very moment everybody seems to have forgotten altogether what was the social use of marriage and to be thinking wholly and solely of the sentimental.

Everything is to be called something that it is not; as in the characteristic example of Companionate Marriage.
(ILN, "The Friends of Frankness, and Euphemism," 6-30-28)

They talk of free love when they mean something quite different, better defined as free lust.

Everybody knows that a man may get tired of a whole procession of immoral women, especially if he is an immoral man.

(TT, ch. 6)

And I suppose it is because the Church has known from the first this weakness which we have all discovered at last, that about certain sexual matters She has been very decisive and dogmatic; as many good people have quite honestly thought, too decisive and dogmatic.

(WEL, "The Surrender Upon Sex")

[see also: Abortion, Abstinence, Birth Control, Chivalry, Contraception, Divorce, Eugenics, Euphemisms, Euthanasia, Family, Feminism, Fidelity, Gender Differences, Home, Marriage, Wives]

Silent Types

They care more for their own manners (a base individualistic asset) than for conversation, which is social, which is impersonal, which is divine.

(ILN, "On Long Speeches and Truth," 2-24-06)

[see also: Cliques, Conversation, Friendship, Neighbors, Singing, Talkers]

Simplicity; Simple Lifestyle

I do not for a moment dream of shielding myself behind so transparent and canting a plea as the notion that there is anything artistic or romantic in being extravagant.

(AWD, "A Sermon on Cheapness" [1902])

But I will have nothing to do with simplicity which lacks the fear, the astonishment, and the joy alike.

I will have nothing to do with the devilish vision of a child who is too simple to like toys.

We need a right view of the human lot, a right view of the human society; and if we were living eagerly and angrily in the enthusiasm of those things, we should, ipso facto, be living simply in the genuine and spiritual sense.

(H, ch. 10)

Judged even by our modern tests of emancipated art or ideal economics, it is admitted that Christ understood all that is rather crudely embodied in Socialism or the Simple Life.

(NJ, ch. 9)

Where the soul really has simplicity it can be grateful for anything—even complexity.

(FVF, ch. 1)

And I for one do not believe that there is any way out of the modern tangle, except to increase the proportion of the people who are living according to the ancient simplicity.

But we must understand things in their simplicity before we can explain or correct their complexity.

(WEL, "Reflections on a Rotten Apple")

[see also: Capitalism, Distributism, Guilds, Philanthropy, Poor, Publicity, Socialism, Thrift, Wealth]

Sin

In the best Utopia, I must be prepared for the moral fall of any man in any position at any moment; especially for my fall from my position at this moment.

(O, ch. 7)

[see also: Angels, Cross, Death, Evil, Ghosts, Incarnation, Jesus, Mary, Mass, Miracles, Morality, Original Sin, Resurrection, Sacramentalism, Saints, Satan & Demons, Transubstantiation, Trinitarianism]

Sincerity

In the modern world solemnity is the direct enemy of sincerity.

(H, ch. 16)

Singing

Once men sang together round a table in chorus; now one man sings alone, for the absurd reason that he can sing better.

(H, ch. 16)

One of the most marked instances of the decline of true popular sympathy is the gradual disappearance in our time of the habit of singing in chorus.

Even when it is done nowadays it is done tentatively and sometimes inaudibly; apparently upon some preposterous principle (which I have never clearly grasped) that singing is an art.

In the new aristocracy of the drawing-room a lady is actually asked whether she sings.

In the old democracy of the dinner table a man was simply told to sing, and he had to do it.

(AD, ch. 38)

[see also: Cliques, Conversation, Friendship, Neighbors, Silent Types, Talkers]

Skepticism (Religious); "Freethinkers"

Opponents of Christianity would believe anything except Christianity.

(ILN, "The Neglect of Christmas," 1-13-06)

For example, one can hardly count the number of times that Christianity has been destroyed or might have been destroyed if its enemies had known where it was or anything about it.

(ILN, "Creed and Deed," 2-2-07)

Nobody supposes that the best critic of music is the man who talks coldly about music.

But there is an idea that a man is a correct judge of religion because he looks down on religions.

(ILN, "The History of Religions," 10-10-08)

If you are merely a sceptic, you must sooner or later ask yourself the question, "Why should *anything* go right; even observation and deduction?

But the old sceptic, the complete sceptic, says, "I have no right to think for myself. I have no right to think at all."

But the new sceptic is so humble that he doubts if he can even learn.

As a politician, he will cry out that war is a waste of life, and then, as a philosopher, that all life is waste of time.

(O, ch. 3)

One rationalist had hardly done calling Christianity a nightmare before another began to call it a fool's paradise.

It looked not so much as if Christianity was bad enough to include any vices, but rather as if any stick was good enough to beat Christianity with.

But if this mass of mad contradictions really existed, quakerish and bloodthirsty, too gorgeous and too threadbare, austere, yet pandering preposterously to the lust of the eye, the enemy of women and their foolish refuge, a solemn pessimist and a silly optimist, if this evil existed, then there was in this evil something quite supreme and unique.

Perhaps, after all, it is Christianity that is sane and all its critics that are mad—in various ways.

(O, ch. 6)

Men who begin to fight the Church for the sake of freedom and humanity end by flinging away freedom and humanity if only they may fight the Church.

(O, ch. 8)

The sceptic is too credulous; he believes in newspapers or even in encyclopedias.

The sceptic may truly be said to be topsy-turvy; for his feet are dancing upwards in idle ecstacies, while his brain is in the abyss.

(O, ch. 9)

Instead of trying to break up new fields with its plough, it simply tries to break up the plough.

(ILN, "Hangmen and Capital Punishment," 2-6-09)

I will not engage in verbal controversy with the sceptic, because long experience has taught me that the sceptic's ultimate skepticism is about the use of his own words and the reliability of his own intelligence.

(ILN, "Objections to Spiritualism," 10-30-09)

It is the decisive people who have become civilised; it is the indecisive, otherwise called the higher sceptics, or the idealistic doubters, who have remained barbarians.

(ILN, "Civilization and Progress," 11-30-12)

Moreover, while it is rare for a great legend to grow out of nothing, it is much easier for a sceptical theory to be woven out of nothing, or next to nothing.

(ILN, "The Legends of Merlin," 9-8-23)

But the people now calling themselves freethinkers are of all thinkers the least free.

In order to explain the opinion of their opponents, they have to deny them the right to hold any opinion at all; and explain away all opinions by servile necessities of the hereditary mentality or the sub-conscious mind.

(ILN, "The Reason For Fear," 2-27-26)

What is now called free thought is valued, not because it is free thought, but because it is freedom from thought; because it is free thoughtlessness.

(CCC, ch. 4)

The person whose position is perpetually growing shaky, shifting, sliding, and breaking away from under him, is the advanced sceptic who is attacking the tradition of orthodoxy.

(ILN, "The Crumbling of the Creeds," 11-26-27)

To begin with, we can hardly be surprised if the Bible-Smasher had never read the Bible, because the Bible-Reader had never read the Bible either.

(ILN, "The Bible and the Sceptics," 4-20-29)

<u>What I think has really happened, in the case of
the more sophisticated youth of today, is that they have
become skeptical of everything, including skepticism.</u>
(ILN, "The Sophistication—and Simplicity—of the
Young," 5-18-29)

The sceptic, like the schoolboy with a penknife, is
always ready to start making a small crack in some of
the planks of the platform of civilization; but he has not
really the courage to split it from end to end.
(ILN, "Mr. Darrow on Divorce," 10-19-29)

<u>For what strikes me most about the skeptics, who
are praised as daring and audacious, is that they dare not
carry out any of their own acts of audacity.</u>
(ILN, "The Modern Recoil From the Modern," 11-9-29)

The truth is that the first questions asked by the sceptic sometimes have an air of intelligence; but if the sceptic
has no answer, or only a negative answer, the silence that
follows soon becomes the very negation of intelligence.

<u>In short, there came to be an entirely false associa-
tion between intelligence and skepticism.</u>
(ILN, "A Defense of Human Dignity," 2-22-30)

How much longer are we expected to put up with
people who have no arguments whatever, beyond the
assertion that religion requires them to believe "what no
intelligent man can accept," or "what thinking people can
no longer regard as rational"?

But what are we to say of the superior philosophical
sceptic, who can only begin the controversy by calling the

other controversialist a fool, and in the same moment end the controversy because he need not controvert with fools?
(ILN, "The Creeds and the Modernist," 5-17-30)

There are very few sceptics in history who cannot be proved to have been instantly swallowed by some swollen convention or some hungry humbug of the hour, so that all their utterances about contemporary things now look to us almost pathetically contemporary.
(WEL, "The Well and the Shallows")

What has troubled me about sceptics all my life has been their extraordinary slowness in coming to the point; even to the point of their own position.

I have heard them denounced, as well as admired, for their headlong haste and reckless rush of innovation; but my difficulty has always been to get them to move a few inches and finish their own argument.
(A, ch. 16)

[see also: Agnosticism, Atheism, Authority, Darwinism, Determinism, Hedonism, "Higher Criticism," Liberalism (Theological), Materialism, Modernism, Physics (Modern), Pragmatism, Progress (Idea of), Rebellion, Science, Secularism, Utopias]

Socialism; Marxism; Communism

Thousands of modern men move quietly and conventionally among their fellows while holding views of national limitation or landed property that would have made Voltaire shudder like a nun listening to blasphemies.
(TWE, ch. 10)

Thus, hundreds of people become Socialists, not because they have tried Socialism and found it nice, but because they have tried Individualism and found it particularly nasty.

(AD, ch. 21)

My own sympathies are with the Socialists; in so far that there is something to be said for Socialism, and nothing to be said for Capitalism.

(NJ, ch. 1)

At one time I agreed with Socialism, because it was simple.

Now I disagree with Socialism, because it is too simple.

The Socialist system, in a more special sense than any other, is founded not on optimism but on original sin.

It proposes that the State, as the conscience of the community, should possess all primary forms of property; and that obviously on the ground that men cannot be trusted to own or barter or combine or compete without injury to themselves.

(EUG, II-7)

Why in the world did Marx tell men they were mechanical dolls at the very moment when he wanted them to behave like martyrs or like murderers?

(ILN, "The Modern Longing For Slavery," 9-15-23)

Bolshevism and every shade of any such theory of brotherhood is based upon one unfathomably mystical Catholic dogma; the equality of men.

(CCC, ch. 4)

It is a remote Utopian dream impossible of fulfilment and also an overwhelming practical danger that threatens us at every moment.

(OS, ch. 1)

[see also: Anarchy, Aristocracy, Caesaropapism, Capitalism, Democracy, Distributism, Government, Guilds, Liberalism (Political), Nazism, Philanthropy, Poor, Revolution, Simplicity, Spain (Civil War), Tolerance, Wealth]

Sociology; Social Problems

If a man wishes to know the origin of human society, to know what society, philosophically speaking, really is, let him not go into the British Museum; let him go into society.

Science can analyse a pork-chop, and say how much of it is phosphorus and how much is protein; but science cannot analyse any man's wish for a pork-chop, and say how much of it is hunger, how much custom, how much nervous fancy, how much a haunting love of the beautiful.

All attempts, therefore, at a science of any human things, at a science of history, a science of folk-lore, a science of sociology, are by their nature not merely hopeless, but crazy.

(H, ch. 11)

Cheap and pedantic prophesying is the curse and the characteristic weakness of the whole of modern sociology.

It is all based on the assumption that man's future can be calculated like the action of a machine; whereas to be incalculable is the definition of being human; it is only because a man cannot be made a subject of science that there is any fun in being a man.
(ILN, "The Impossibility of Altering the 'System',"
2-9-07)

But social science is by no means always content with the normal human soul; it has all sorts of fancy souls for sale.

But exactly the whole difficulty in our public problems is that some men are aiming at cures which other men would regard as worse maladies; are offering ultimate conditions as states of health which others would uncompromisingly call states of disease.

The only way to discuss the social evil is to get at once to the social ideal.

What is wrong is that we do not ask what is right.
(WWW, I-1)

It is only with great difficulty that a modern scientific sociologist can be got to see that any old method has a leg to stand on.
(WWW, III-2)

The trouble with most sociologists, criminologists, etc., is that while their knowledge of their own details is exhaustive and subtle, their knowledge of man and society, to which these are to be applied, is quite exceptionally superficial and silly.

(AD, ch. 13)

By experts in poverty I do not mean sociologists, but poor men.

(ILN, "A Nightmare of Nonsense," 3-25-11)

[see also: Anthropology, Ceremony, Compartmentalization, Customs, Environment, Family, Feminism, Gender Differences, Home, Man, Man (Smallness of), Marriage, Nationality, Sexuality]

Sola Scriptura (Scripture as Infallible Authority)

But in what conceivable frame of mind does he rush in to select one particular scroll of the scriptures of this one particular group (a scroll which had always belonged to them and been a part of their hocus-pocus, if it was hocus-pocus); why in the world should the man in the street say that one particular scroll was not bosh, but was the one and only truth by which all the other things were to be condemned?

Why should it not be as reasonable to preserve the statues as the scrolls, by the tenets of that particular creed?

To say, "Your statues are condemned by your scrolls, and we are going to worship one part of your procession and wreck the rest," is not sensible from any standpoint, least of all that of the man in the street.

(CCC, ch. 2)

To an impartial pagan or sceptical observer, it must always seem the strangest story in the world; that men rushing in to wreck a temple, overturning the altar and driving out the priest, found there certain sacred volumes inscribed "Psalms" or "Gospels"; and (instead of throwing them on the fire with the rest) began to use them as infallible oracles rebuking all the other arrangements.

(TT, ch. 3)

The Puritans thought they were simplifying things by appealing to what they called the plain words of Scripture; but as a fact they were complicating things by bringing in half a hundred cranky sects and crazy suggestions.

(TT, ch. 30)

[see also: Bible, "Higher Criticism," Private Judgment, Prophets, Protestantism, Revelation (Book of)]

Spain; Civil War in

<u>And then the Socialists suddenly jumped up and did exactly everything that the Fascists have been blamed for doing.</u>

Having lost the game by the rules of democracy, they tried to win it after all entirely by the rules of war; in this case of Civil War.

In short, they behaved exactly like Mussolini; or rather they did the very worst that has ever been attributed to Mussolini; and without a rag of his theoretical excuse.

The only inference was that Liberalism was only opposed to militarists when they were Fascists; and entirely approved of Fascists so long as they were Socialists.

(WEL, "The Case of Spain")

Some of them still mumble old memories about the Spanish Inquisition (a thing started strictly by the State); with the fact staring them in the face that the actual persecution now going on in Spain is the spoliation of Spaniards, simply because they are Catholic priests and schoolmasters.

(WEL, "The Return of Caesar")

[see also: Anarchy, Democracy, Liberalism (Political), Monarchy, Nationalism, Nazism, Patriotism, Revolution, Socialism, Tolerance]

Spirit of the Age (Zeitgeist)

It is always easy to let the age have its head; the difficult thing is to keep one's own.

(O, ch. 6)

A dead thing can go with the stream, but only a living thing can go against it.

(EM, II-6)

[see also: Conformity, Fashions, Nonconformity (Christian)]

Spiritualism; Occult

Spirits are not worth all this fuss; I know that, for I am one myself.
(ILN, "Scepticism About Spiritualism," 4-14-06)

They entertain angels unawares – fallen angels.
(ILN, "Objections to Spiritualism," 10-30-09)

Some Pagan gods were lawless, and some Christian saints were a little too serious; but the spirits of modern spiritualism are both lawless and serious—a disgusting combination.
(TRE, ch. 17)

Spiritualism also has the trend of polytheism, if it be in a form more akin to ancestor-worship.

I am merely describing the drift of the day; and it seems clear that it is towards the summoning of spirits to our aid whatever their position in the unknown world, and without any clear doctrinal plan of that world.

The most probable result would seem to be a multitude of psychic cults, personal and impersonal, from the vaguest reverence for the powers of nature to the most concrete appeal to crystals or mascots.
(NJ, ch. 8)

There has been a revolt against Christian morality, and where there has not been a return of Christian mysticism, it has been a return of the mysticism without the Christianity.

Mysticism itself has returned, with all its moons and twilights, its talismans and spells.

Mysticism itself has returned, and brought with it seven devils worse than itself.

(NJ, ch. 9)

The spiritualist is nearly always a converted materialist.

(ILN, "The Blank State of the Modern Mind," 4-3-26)

They are, as it were, people just educated enough to have heard of ghosts but not educated enough to have heard of witches.

(CCC, ch. 4)

I have since come to think, for reasons that would require too much space to detail, that it is not so much supernatural as unnatural and even anti-natural.

(CCC, ch. 5)

[see also: Angels, Death, Ghosts, Gnosticism, Heresies, Orthodoxy, Paganism, Reincarnation, Religion (Comparative), Satan & Demons, Superstition]

Stories

The 'Iliad' is only great because all life is a battle, the 'Odyssey' because all life is a journey, the Book of Job because all life is a riddle.

(DEF, ch. 5)

That is because a story has behind it, not merely intellect which is partly mechanical, but will, which is in its essence divine.

(H, ch. 14)

But the essential on which I should insist would be, not that the tale must be true, but that the tale must be fine.

(ILN, "History and Inspiration," 10-8-10)

The only two things that can satisfy the soul are a person and a story; and even a story must be about a person.

(MM, ch. 15)

[see also: Adventure, Children, Fairy Tales, Fiction, Imagination, Mythology, Nature, Novels, Romanticism, Wonder]

Suicide

It is the ultimate and absolute evil, the refusal to take an interest in existence; the refusal to take the oath of loyalty to life.

A suicide is a man who cares so little for anything outside him, that he wants to see the last of everything.

(O, ch. 5)

[see also: Despair, Fanatics, Madness, Moods, Optimism, Pessimism, Resignation]

Superstition

I doubt if any one century is much more superstitious than any other century.

In so far as there is a slight difference, the twentieth century is more superstitious than the nineteenth century; and the twenty-first century (to all appearance) will be more superstitious than the twentieth.
(ILN, "Superstition and Modern Justice," 10-6-06)

The Church has been superstitious: but it has never been so superstitious as the world is when left to itself.
(ILN, "Francis Thompson and Religious Poetry," 12-14-07)

Superstition recurs in all ages, and especially in rationalistic ages.

(EM, I-5)

The age we live in is something more than an age of superstition—it is an age of innumerable superstitions.

(EUG, I-7)

[see also: Gnosticism, Heresies, Modernism, Orthodoxy, Paganism, Reincarnation, Religion (Comparative), Spiritualism]

Talkers

It is an entire mistake, for instance, to imagine that the man who monopolises conversation is a conceited fellow.

The man who talks too much, talks too much because he is interested in his subject.

He is not interested in himself: if he were he would behave better.

(ILN, "On Long Speeches and Truth," 2-24-06)

[see also: Cliques, Conversation, Friendship, Neighbors, Silent Types, Singing]

Taste, Matters of

Thus it is considered more withering to accuse a man of bad taste than of bad ethics.

(TRE, ch. 10)

A dispute about taste is never in any sense settled.
(ILN, "Disputes About Artistic Tastes," 12-17-27)

Everything has become a matter of opinion, or, rather, a matter of taste; and larger and larger crowds of people simply have a taste in quacks.
(ILN, "Twilight Sleep and the Breakdown of Reason," 11-2-29)

Temper

Unfortunately, good temper is sometimes more irritating than bad temper.
(STA, ch. 7)

Temptation

Christianity never said that man had outlived temptation or that science was an antiseptic against sin.
(ILN, "Lord Birkenhead's Attack on Idealism," 12-1-23)

[see also: Asceticism, Confession, Faith, Incense, Martyrdom, Mysticism, Relics, Robes, Sabbath, Satan & Demons]

Theism, Monotheism, and Polytheism

The riddles of God are more satisfying than the solutions of man.
(JOB)

I had always felt life first as a story: and if there is a story there is a story-teller.
(O, ch. 4)

By insisting specially on the transcendence of God we get wonder, curiosity, moral and political adventure, righteous indignation—Christendom.

(O, ch. 8)

The essence of polytheism is the worship of gods who are not God; that is, who are not necessarily the author and the authority of all things.

(NJ, ch. 8)

Polytheism fades away at its fringes into fairy-tales or barbaric memories; it is not a thing like monotheism as held by serious monotheists.

(EM, I-5)

[see also: Agnosticism, Apologetics, Argument, Atheism, Creation, Faith (and Reason), Ideas, Idealism, Paradox (in Christianity), Materialism, Philosophy, Reason & Logic, Science (and Religion), Truth]

Theologians

To have a theology is our only protection against the wicked restlessness of theologians.

(ILN, "The Need of Doctrine in the Church," 10-27-06)

But just as the physiologist is dealing with living tissues, so the theologian is dealing with living ideas; and if he draws a line between them it is naturally a very fine line.

(TT, ch. 29)

[see also: Authority (Religious), Catholicism & Catholics, Catholicity, Christianity, Church (Catholic), Conversion (Catholic), Development (Doctrinal), Dogma (Catholic),

"Higher Criticism," History (Church), Liberalism (Religious), Modernism, Orthodoxy, Paganism (and Christianity), Papacy & Popes, Protestantism, Reformation (Catholic), Religion (Organized), Skepticism, Tradition]

Thrift

Thrift is the really romantic thing; economy is more romantic than extravagance.

Thrift is poetic because it is creative; waste is unpoetic because it is waste.

It is prosaic to throw money away, because it is prosaic to throw anything away; it is negative; it is a confession of indifference, that is, it is a confession of failure.

If a man could undertake to make use of all things in his dustbin he would be a broader genius than Shakespeare.

For in the average human house there is one hole by which money comes in and a hundred by which it goes out; man has to do with the one hole, woman with the hundred.

(WWW, III-4)

A miser is a man who is intercepted and misled in his pursuit of thrift and betrayed into turning to the pursuit of money.

(AS, ch. 26)

[see also: Capitalism, Distributism, Guilds, Philanthropy, Poor, Publicity, Simplicity, Socialism, Wealth]

Tolerance and Persecution

We think that we are more tolerant because we do
not any longer burn people.

(ILN, "Bigotry in the Modern World," 4-28-06)

Religious persecution does not consist in thumbscrews or fires of Smithfield; the essence of religious
persecution is this: that the man who happens to have
material power in the State, either by wealth or by
official position, should govern his fellow-citizens not
according to their religion or philosophy, but according
to his own.

(ATC, ch. 1)

Not only was it then the Catholics who were proposing toleration, but it was they who had already actually
established toleration in the State of Maryland, before
the Puritans began to establish the most intolerant sort
of intolerance in the State of New England.

(FVF, ch. 23)

For the modern mind is merely a blank about the
philosophy of toleration; and the average agnostic of
recent times has really had no notion of what he meant
by religious liberty and equality.

(SF, ch. 8)

[see also: Anarchy, Bigotry & Racism, Broadmindedness, Caesaropapism, Democracy, Dogmatism, Government, Law, Liberalism (Political), Nazism, Openmindedness, Prejudice, Revolution, Socialism, Spain (Civil War),
Tolerance]

Tradition

It is obvious that tradition is only democracy extended through time.

It is the democracy of the dead.

(O, ch. 4)

I was always rushing out of my architectural study with plans for a new turret only to find it sitting up there in the sunlight, shining, and a thousand years old.

(O, ch. 7)

Tradition is not a dry and dusty and antiquated affair.

The tradition, as a matter of fact, has come down through numberless generations; but each person remembers it by the person who had it last.

He does not think of it as a thing connected with his first forefathers; but as a thing connected with his father.

(ILN, "The Age of Antiquities," 11-19-10)

Why do we find today this vast and vague mass of trivialities, which have nothing in common except that they are *all* in reaction against the very best of human traditions?

I am wondering what has debased the currency of current though and speech, and why every normal ideal of man is now pelted with handfuls of such valueless pebbles, and assailed everywhere, not by free thought, but by frank thoughtlessness.

(AIS, ch. 44)

[see also: Authority (Religious), Catholicism & Catholics, Catholicity, Christianity, Church (Catholic), Conversion (Catholic), Development (Doctrinal), Dogma (Catholic), History (Church), Orthodoxy, Paganism (and Christianity), Papacy & Popes, Protestantism, Reformation (Catholic), Religion (Organized), Theologians]

Traffic Congestion

The great social reform of the Prohibition of Petrol would certainly relieve the congestion very much; and for that and many other reasons I look confidently to Mr. Ford to give it his eager and enthusiastic support.

(ILN, "Mr. Ford and Prohibition," 5-22-26)

In fact, I fear I never like the traffic quite so much as when it stands still.

In the middle of a prolonged block in the Uxbridge Road, I have been known to exhibit a gaiety and radiant levity which has made me loathed and detested for miles round.

I always feel a faint hope, after a few hours of it, that the vehicles may never move on at all; but may sink slowly into the road and take on the more rooted character of a large and prosperous village.

(AIS, ch. 4)

[see also: Automobiles, Capitalism, Cities, Communications, Hustle & Bustle, Inventions]

Transubstantiation

As to Transubstantiation, it is less easy to talk currently about that; but I would gently suggest that, to most ordinary outsiders with any common sense, there would be a considerable practical difference between Jehovah pervading the universe and Jesus Christ coming into the room.

(TT, ch. 7)

[see also: Angels, Cross, Death, Evil, Ghosts, Incarnation, Jesus, Mary, Mass, Miracles, Original Sin, Resurrection, Sacramentalism, Saints, Satan & Demons, Sin, Trinitarianism]

Travel

There are no dreary sights; there are only dreary sightseers.

(AD, ch. 39)

But the general spirit of travel, the desire to see new folk or new customs, all that has been ruined by the commercial concentration of modern times.

(ILN, "The Meaning of Travel," 10-2-26)

Trinitarianism

For to us Trinitarians (if I may say it with reverence)—to us God Himself is a society.

(O, ch. 8)

Even in the days of my youth, I remarked that there was something slightly odd about despising and dismissing the doctrine of the Trinity as a mystical and even maniacal contradiction; and then asking us to adore a deity who is a hundred million persons in one God, neither confounding the persons nor dividing the substance.

(EM, I-4)

[see also: Angels, Cross, Death, Evil, Ghosts, Incarnation, Jesus, Mary, Mass, Miracles, Original Sin, Resurrection, Sacramentalism, Saints, Satan & Demons, Sin, Transubstantiation]

Truth

Men can believe anything, even the truth.

(ILN, "Fancies and Facts," 9-22-06)

A man was meant to be doubtful about himself, but undoubting about the truth; this has been exactly reversed.

(O, ch. 3)

But the evidence in my case, as in that of the intelligent agnostic, is not really in this or that alleged demonstration; it is in an enormous accumulation of small but unanimous facts.

(O, ch. 9)

A man who thinks hard about any subject for several years is in horrible danger of discovering the truth about it.

(ILN, "Adjectives, Nouns, and the Truth," 10-16-09)

The whole truth is generally the ally of virtue; a half-truth is always the ally of some vice.

(ILN, "The Collapse of the Victorian Compromise,"
6-11-10)

But no English school-boy is ever taught to tell the truth, for the very simple reason that he is never taught to desire the truth.

(WWW, IV-11)

The test of true religion is that its energy drives exactly the other way; it is always trying to make men feel truths as facts; always trying to make abstract things as plain and solid as concrete things; always trying to make men, not merely admit the truth, but see, smell, handle, hear, and devour the truth.

(AD, ch. 7)

This weakness in civilisation is best expressed by saying that it cares more for science than for truth.

(MM, ch. 28)

There can be no doubt about it for any one who can apply as a test the truth I have mentioned; that the fundamental things in a man are not the things he explains, but rather the things he forgets to explain.

(SD, ch. 3)

Perhaps there are no things out of which we get so little of the truth as the truisms; especially when they are really true.

(EM, I-6)

One word that tells us what we do not know outweighs a thousand words that tell us what we do know.

(CCC, ch. 5)

Public opinion, taken as a whole is much more contemptuous of specialists and seekers after truth than the Church ever was.

(TT, ch. 13)

I could never at any time understand why there is supposed to be something insolent or intolerant about a man asserting that he has the Truth, and therefore proposes to persuade as many people as possible that it is the Truth.

(ILN, "The Menace of Spiritualism," 8-16-30)

Those who leave the tradition of truth do not escape into something which we call Freedom.

(WEL, "The Well and the Shallows")

If I had wandered away like Bergson or Bernard Shaw, and made up my own philosophy out of my own precious fragment of truth, merely because I had found it for myself, I should soon have found that truth distorting itself into a falsehood.

(A, ch. 16)

[see also: Apologetics, Argument, Faith (and Reason), Ideas, Idealism, Paradox (in Christianity), Philosophy, Reason & Logic, Science (and Religion), Theism]

𝒰

Utopias

The skeptical theorist is allowed to throw off Utopia after Utopia, and is never reproached when they are contradicted by the facts, or contradicted by each other.

(ILN, "Buddhism and Christianity," 3-2-29)

"Values"

I can see the value of "values," but I wish we had proved ourselves more worthy of a strong and sound word like "worth."

(ILN, "Keeping Old Words New," 8-28-26)

Vegetarianism

Meat-eating is either not wrong at all (as I think), or it is very wrong.

(ILN, "Bigotry in the Modern World," 4-28-06)

How can I denounce a man for skinning cats, if he is only now what I may possibly become in drinking a glass of milk?

(O, ch. 7)

Then, of course, there is the larger and more philosophic riddle of why the vegetarians, or fruitarians, try to
make their dishes sound, or even seem, like meat dishes?

If they really think it wrong to eat meat, if they honestly
consider it a kind of cannibalism, why should they introduce
reminders of the revolting habit they have renounced?
(ILN, "Honesty in Vegetarianism," 12-4-09)

[see also: Abortion, Animal Rights, Environmentalism, Euthanasia, Man, Morality]

Vernacular

But while I see what there is to be said for the cult
of the vernacular, the Protestant critic does not see what
there is to be said for the fixed form of the classic tongue.
(TT, ch. 26)

[see also: Language, Mass]

Victorianism

For instance, I find some people so astonishingly
ignorant as to class theology or religious dogma as surviv-
als of Victorian England, of which by far the most unmis-
takable mark was that general recognition of doubt and
agnosticism, expressed vigorously in Huxley and gracefully in Matthew Arnold.
(ILN, "The Victorians and the Moderns," 8-13-27)

There was much in Victorian ideas that I dislike
and much that I respect; but there was nothing whatever

about Victorian ideas corresponding to what is now called Victorian.

(A, ch. 6)

[see also: Empires, History]

Voting

But voting ought not to mean this: voting ought to mean arguing for hours and hours in a public-house and interrupting people and hitting the table.

(ILN, "Female Suffrage and the New Theology," 3-16-07)

The average man votes below himself; he votes with half a mind or with a hundredth part of one.

A man ought to vote with the whole of himself as he worships or gets married.

The point is that only a minority of the voter votes.

(TRE, ch. 35)

They cannot have what they choose, but only which they choose.

(MM, ch. 7)

[see also: Anarchy, Democracy, Government, Law, Patriotism, Politicians]

Vows

The man who makes a vow makes an appointment with himself at some distant time or place.

(DEF, ch. 2)

The shortest way of putting the problem is to ask whether being free includes being free to bind oneself.

For the vow is a tryst with oneself.

(SD, ch. 1)

It is to combine the fixity that goes with finality with the self-respect that only goes with freedom.

(SD, ch. 6)

Vulgarity

When somebody tries to impress us, either with his wit or assurance, or knowledge of the world, or power, or grace, or even poetry and ideality, and in the very act of doing so shows he has low ideas of all these things – that is Vulgarity.

(ILN, "A Definition of Vulgarity," 6-8-29)

In practice it means handling things confidently and contemptuously, without the sense that all things in their way are sacred things.

(CM, "Vulgarity")

WXYZ

Walking

The objects of a walk are often disappointing, but the accidents are magnificent.

Upon the whole, it may be admitted that the pedestrian should carry a map, but he should not consult it often, and he should always cherish the thrilling and secret thought that it may be all wrong.

In fact, a map should be taken chiefly because it is such a particularly beautiful thing in itself.

A walking tour, for example, is unthinkable without a walking-stick, though the experienced will have the strongest internal doubts whether it is any use, and the walking-stick of all walking-sticks for such a purpose is one cut in the woods, as being the most rough and crooked and inconvenient.

Carrying such a staff a man feels himself a thing of the earth.

The essential ground of the unwisdom and unprofitableness of planning a walk too systematically with maps and guide books is a thing easy to feel, but not quite so easy to analyse.

(AWD, "Walking Tours" [1901])

To begin with, if there were no petrol traffic, there is always the possibility that Americans might learn to walk.

(ILN, "Mr. Ford and Prohibition," 5-22-26)

Wallpaper

I could not understand why one arbitrary symbol (a symbol apparently entirely devoid of any religious or philosophical significance) should thus be sprinkled all over my nice walls like a sort of small-pox.

The Bible must be referring to wallpapers, I think, when it says, "Use not vain repetitions, as the Gentiles do."

(TRE, ch. 10)

War

In matters of battle and conquest we have got firmly rooted in our minds the idea (an idea fit for the philosophers of Bedlam) that we can best trample on a people by ignoring all the particular merits which give them a chance of trampling upon us.

It has become a breach of etiquette to praise the enemy; whereas when the enemy is strong every honest scout ought to praise the enemy.

It is impossible to vanquish an army without having a full account of its strength.

(TWE, ch. 4)

All ages and all epics have sung of arms and the man; but we have effected simultaneously the deterioration of the man and the fantastic perfection of the arms.

(H, ch. 3)

There must be *some* good in the life of battle, for so many good men have enjoyed being soldiers.

(O, ch. 6)

The true soldier fights not because he hates what is in front of him, but because he loves what is behind him.

(ILN, "Christmas and Disarmament," 1-14-11)

War is not the best way of settling differences; it is the only way of preventing their being settled for you.

(ILN, "German Evil and English Weaknesses," 7-24-15)

[see also: Pacifism, War (and Christianity), World War I]

War (and Christianity)

The very people who reproached Christianity with the meekness and non-resistance of the monasteries were the very people who reproached it also with the violence and valour of the Crusades.

The Quakers (we were told) were the only characteristic Christians; and yet the massacres of Cromwell and Alva were characteristic Christian crimes.

(O, ch. 6)

As for the general view that the Church was discredited by the War—they might as well say that the Ark was discredited by the Flood.

(EM, Introduction)

I do not know whether Martin Luther invented mustard gas, or George Fox manufactured tear-shells, or St. Thomas Aquinas devised a stink-bomb producing suffocation.

If wars are the horrid fruits of a thing called Christianity, they are also the horrid fruits of everything called citizenship and democracy and liberty and national independence, and are we to judge all these and condemn them by their fruits?

Anyhow such a modern war is much greater than any of the wars that can be referred to religious motives, or even religious epochs.

The broad truth about the matter is that wars have become more organised, and more ghastly in the particular period of Materialism.

(ILN, "The Guilt of the Churches," 7-26-30)

Properly speaking, the only rational wars are the religious wars.

If a man may be asked to die for anything, it may well be for his whole reason for living, his whole conception of the object of life and death.

(ILN, "The Only Rational Wars," 9-26-31)

[see also: Crusades, Hypocrisy (of Christians), Inquisition, Pacifism, War (and Christianity), World War I]

Wealth and Wealthy Men

And the reason why the lives of the rich are at bottom so tame and uneventful is simply that they can choose the events.

They are dull because they are omnipotent.

They fail to feel adventures because they can make the adventures.

(H, ch. 14)

We are always talking about the sin of intemperate drinking, because it is quite obvious that the poor have it more than the rich.

But we are always denying that there is any such thing as the sin of pride, because it would be quite obvious that the rich have it more than the poor.

(H, ch. 19)

Wealth has a distinctly barbarising tendency.

But when the bodies of six rich men sit side by side, their souls do not sit side by side at all.

(ILN, "The Millionaires' Freak Dinner," 3-24-06)

But the rich are not content with changing their creeds as often as their bonnets; they always want to preach each one of these vanishing visions to the people under their control.

(ILN, "The Mad Philanthropist, Again," 12-22-06)

If prosperity is regarded as the reward of virtue it will be regarded as the symptom of virtue.

(JOB)

Only the Christian Church can offer any rational objection to a complete confidence in the rich.

But if we diminish the camel to his smallest, or open the eye of the needle to its largest—if, in short, we assume the words of Christ to have meant the very least that they could mean, His words must at the very least mean this—that rich men are not very likely to be morally trustworthy.

For the whole modern world is absolutely based on the assumption, not that the rich are necessary (which is tenable), but that the rich are trustworthy, which (for a Christian) is not tenable.

The whole case for Christianity is that a man who is dependent upon the luxuries of this life is a corrupt man, spiritually corrupt, politically corrupt, financially corrupt.

But it is quite certainly un-Christian to trust the rich, to regard the rich as more morally safe than the poor.

(O, ch. 7)

For if comfort gives men virtue, the comfortable classes ought to be virtuous—which is absurd.

(TRE, ch. 32)

In short, the rich are always modern; it is their business.

(WWW, I-10)

The typical modern man is the insane millionaire who has drudged to get money, and then finds he cannot enjoy even money.

(AWD, "What is Right With the World" [1910])

What is deadly dull about the millionaire-banquets is that there is a contrast between colossal resources and no idea.

(AD, ch. 31)

But among the Very Rich you will never find a really generous man, even by accident.

They may give their money away, but they will never give themselves away; they are egoistic, secretive, dry as old bones.

To be smart enough to get all that money you must be dull enough to want it.

(MM, ch. 20)

The modern English rich know nothing about things, not even about the things to which they appeal.

(UTO, "The Empire of the Ignorant")

In all intense religions it is the poor who are more religious and the rich who are more irreligious.

(NJ, ch. 7)

I should say that no rich man in the past ever had anything like the power over humanity possessed by a millionaire or financier to-day.

But some of us think there are still evidences of that evil power of Mammon which called for the challenge of St. Francis.

(ILN, "Power, Mediaeval and Modern," 5-29-26)

It is no longer Liberty against Luxury, but Liberty for the sake of Luxury.

(ILN, "Liberty, Liberalism, and the Libertarians," 3-3-28)

The millionaire leaves his money to other millionaires.
(ILN, "The New Immoral Philosophy," 9-21-29)

[see also: Aristocracy, Capitalism, Distributism,
Guilds, Philanthropy, Poor, Publicity, Simplicity, Socialism, Thrift]

Weather

I do not know if other people are made like me in this
matter; but to me it is always dreary weather, what may
be called useless weather, that slings into life a sense of
action and romance.

(TRE, ch. 3)

And if it is exciting when a man throws a pail of
water over you, why should it not also be exciting when
the gods throw many pails?

(TRE, ch. 38)

Two men should share an umbrella; if they have not
got an umbrella, they should at least share the rain, with
all its rich potentialities of wit and philosophy.

This is the second element in the weather; its
recognition of human equality in that we all have our
hats under the dark blue spangled umbrella of the
universe.

All true friendliness begins with fire and food and
drink and the recognition of rain or frost.

(WWW, II-2)

But for my part I will praise the English climate till I die—even if I die of the English climate.

Only in our own romantic country do you have the strictly romantic thing called Weather; beautiful and changing as a woman.

(AD, ch. 18)

Spring never is Spring unless it comes too soon.

(MM, ch. 6)

The enthusiastic water drinker must regard a rainstorm as a sort of universal banquet and debauch of his own favourite beverage.

Shut up, an umbrella is an unmanageable walking-stick; open, it is an inadequate tent.

For my part, I have no taste for pretending to be a walking pavilion; I think nothing of my hat, and precious little of my head.

(MM, ch. 27)

I do not dislike snow; on the contrary I delight in it; and if it had drifted as deep in my own country against my own door I should have thought it the triumph of Christmas, and a thing as comic as my own dog and donkey.

(NJ, ch. 5)

We can no more subject the world to the English compromise than to the English climate; and both are things of incalculable cloud and twilight.

A London fog is tolerable in London, indeed I think it is very enjoyable in London.

(NJ, ch. 7)

Will

Exactly as complete free thought involves the doubting of thought itself, so the acceptation of mere "willing" really paralyzes the will.

So he who wills to reject nothing, wills the destruction of will; for will is not only the choice of something, but the rejection of almost everything.

(O, ch. 3)

Wit

A man may pretend to be a poet: he can no more pretend to be a wit than he can pretend to bring rabbits out of a hat without having learnt to be a conjurer.

(TWE, ch. 4)

There is considerable difference between a wit making a fool of himself and a fool making a wit of himself.

(AD, ch. 31)

Wit is reason on its judgment seat; and though the offenders may be touched lightly, the point is that the judge is not touched at all.

(SL, "Humour" [1918])

There is such a thing as sham wisdom; but there cannot be any such thing as sham wit.
(ILN, "A Defense of the Neo-Classical Poets," 3-27-26)

When the question merely hung unanswered in the air, in a restless, worldly, and uncontemplative age, there came to be a vague association between wit and that sort of sneering inquiry.
(ILN, "A Defense of Human Dignity," 2-22-30)

[see also: Fools, Hilarity, Humor, Satire]

Wives

I never met a wife who did not know all the weaknesses of her husband and count on them as calmly as she counted on sunrise or the spring.

I really think that the man who has tamed a wife is more exceptional than the man who has tamed a tiger or a chimpanzee; and also much more unpleasant.

The normal man is much more afraid of his wife than his wife is afraid of him.
(ILN, "Listening to Modernist Arguments," 8-29-08)

The same women who are ready to defend their men through thick and thin are (in their personal intercourse with the man) almost morbidly lucid about the thinness of his excuses or the thickness of his head.

A man's friend likes him but leaves him as he is: his wife loves him and is always trying to turn him into somebody else.

(O, ch. 5)

But there is no hope for men who do not boast that their wives bully them.

(AD, ch. 5)

Variability is one of the virtues of a woman.

(AD, ch. 18)

[see also: Abortion, Abstinence, Birth Control, Contraception, Divorce, Eugenics, Euphemisms, Euthanasia, Family, Feminism, Fidelity, Gender Differences, Home, Marriage, Sexuality]

Wonder

The curse that came before history has laid on us all a tendency to be weary of wonders.

Until we understand that original dark, in which we have neither sight nor expectation, we can give no hearty and childlike praise to the splendid sensationalism of things.

(H, ch. 12)

The world will never starve for want of wonders; but only for want of wonder.

(TRE, ch. 1)

[see also: Adventure, Children, Fairy Tales, Imagination, Mysticism, Mythology, Nature, Romanticism, Stories]

Work; Labor

If reapers sing while reaping, why should not auditors sing while auditing and bankers while banking?

(TRE, ch. 30)

We rejoice when we find remaining in the world any cases in which the individual can see the beginning and the end of his own work.

(ILN, "Women in the Workplace – and at Home," 12-18-26)

World War I: "The Great War"

It was a war between England as a part of Europe and Prussia as the leader of the barbarism that has always existed on the border of Europe.

(ILN, "Christianity in the Great War," 1-19-24)

[see also: Pacifism, War, War (and Christianity]

Writers

The men who have really been the bold artists, the realistic artists, the uncompromising artists, are the men who have turned out, after all, to be writing "with a purpose."

(H, ch. 20)

For instance, I am staring blankly at this sheet of paper and I firmly believe that something more or less intelligible will happen soon.

(SL, "On Fragments" [1906])

Whereas, as I have only too good reason to know, if you are writing an article you can say anything that comes into your head.

(TRE, ch. 23)

Any man with a large mind ought to be able to write about anything.

Any really free man ought to be able to write to order.

(AWD, "What is Right With the World" [1910])

The morality of a great writer is not the morality he teaches, but the morality he takes for granted.

(SD, ch. 3)

Most people would agree that even good writers can write too much, and that bad writers cannot write too little.

(AIS, ch. 30)

Over and above the horrible rubbish-heap of the books I have written, now filling the pulping-machines or waste-paper baskets of the world, there are a vast number of books that I have never written, because a providential diversion interposed to protect the crowd of my fellow-creatures who could endure no more.

(AS, ch. 1)

If they copy the last century, they are old-fashioned; but if it is quite clear that they are much more than a hundred years old, they are entirely fresh and original.

(AS, ch. 15)

I have never taken my books seriously; but I take my opinions quite seriously.

(A, ch. 5)

[see also: Art and Artists, Fiction, Language, Jargon, Newspapers, Novels, Poetry, Stories]

Bibliography of Sources by Abbreviations

A	*Autobiography* (London: Hutchinson, 1936)
AD	*Alarms And Discursions* (London: Methuen & Co., 1911)
AIS	*All I Survey* (London: Methuen & Co., 1933)
AS	*As I Was Saying* (London: Methuen & Co., 1936)
ATC	*All Things Considered* (London: Methuen & Co., 1908)
AWD	*The Apostle and the Wild Ducks* (London: Paul Elek, 1975)
CCC	*The Catholic Church and Conversion* (London: Burns, Oates & Washbourne, 1926)
CD	*Charles Dickens* (London: Methuen & Co., 1906)
CM	*The Common Man* (New York: Sheed & Ward, 1950)
DEF	*The Defendant* (New York: Dodd, Mead and Co., 1902)
EM	*The Everlasting Man* (New York: Dodd, Mead and Co., 1925)
EUG	*Eugenics and Other Evils* (New York: Dodd, Mead and Co., 1922)
FVF	*Fancies Versus Fads* (London: Methuen, 1923)
GBS	*George Bernard Shaw* (New York: John Lane Co., 1909)
H	*Heretics* (New York: John Lane Co., 1905)
HAT	*On Running After One's Hat and Other Whimsies* (New York: Robert M. McBride & Co., 1933)
ILN	*The Collected Works of G. K. Chesterton: Volume XXVII:* The Illustrated London News: *1905–1907* (edited by Lawrence J. Clipper; San Francisco: Ignatius Press, 1986)
ILN	*The Collected Works of G. K. Chesterton: Volume XXVIII:* The Illustrated London News: *1908–1910* (edited by Lawrence J.

	Clipper; general editors: George J. Marlin, Richard P. Rabatin, and John L. Swan; San Francisco: Ignatius Press, 1987)
ILN	*The Collected Works of G. K. Chesterton: Volume XXIX:* The Illustrated London News: *1911–1913* (edited by Lawrence J. Clipper; general editors: George J. Marlin, Richard P. Rabatin, and John L. Swan; San Francisco: Ignatius Press, 1988)
ILN	*The Collected Works of G. K. Chesterton: Volume XXX:* The Illustrated London News: *1914–1916* (edited by Lawrence J. Clipper; general editors: George J. Marlin, Richard P. Rabatin, and John L. Swan; San Francisco: Ignatius Press, 1988)
ILN	*The Collected Works of G. K. Chesterton: Volume XXXIII:* The Illustrated London News: *1923–1925* (edited by Lawrence J. Clipper; general editors: George J. Marlin, Richard P. Rabatin, and John L. Swan; San Francisco: Ignatius Press, 1990)
ILN	*The Collected Works of G. K. Chesterton: Volume XXXIV:* The Illustrated London News: *1926–1928* (edited by Lawrence J. Clipper; general editors: George J. Marlin, Richard P. Rabatin, and John L. Swan; San Francisco: Ignatius Press, 1991)
ILN	*The Collected Works of G. K. Chesterton: Volume XXXV:* The Illustrated London News: *1929–1931* (edited by Lawrence J. Clipper; general editors: George J. Marlin, Richard P. Rabatin, and John L. Swan; San Francisco: Ignatius Press, 1991)
JOB	*Introduction to the Book of Job* (London: S. Wellwood, 1907)
MM	*A Miscellany of Men* (London: Methuen & Co., 1912)
NJ	*The New Jerusalem* (London: Hodder & Stoughton, 1920)
O	*Orthodoxy* (New York: John Lane Co., 1908)
OS	*The Outline of Sanity* (London: Methuen & Co., 1926)
ROC	*The Return of Christendom* (London: G. Allen & Unwin, 1922) [Epilogue section only]
SD	*The Superstition of Divorce* (New York: John Lane Co., 1920)
SF	*St. Francis of Assisi* (London: Hodder & Stoughton, 1924)
SL	*The Spice of Life and Other Essays* (London: Darwen Finlayson, 1964)
STA	*St. Thomas Aquinas* (London: Hodder & Stoughton, 1933)
TRE	*Tremendous Trifles* (London: Methuen & Co., 1909)
TT	*The Thing: Why I am a Catholic* (New York: Sheed & Ward, 1929)
TWE	*Twelve Types* (London: A.L. Humphreys, 1903)
UTO	*Utopia of Usurers, and Other Essays* (New York: Boni & Liveright, 1917)
VT	*Varied Types* (New York: Dodd, Mead and Co., 1905)
WC	*William Cobbett* (New York: Dodd, Mead and Co., 1926)
WEL	*The Well and The Shallows* (New York: Sheed & Ward, 1935)
WWW	*What's Wrong With the World* (London: Cassell, 1910)

Bibliography of Sources in Chronological Order

1902	DEF *The Defendant* (New York: Dodd, Mead & Co.)
1903	TWE *Twelve Types* (London: A.L. Humphreys)
1905	H *Heretics* (New York: John Lane Co.)
1905	VT *Varied Types* (New York: Dodd, Mead and Co.)
1906	CD *Charles Dickens* (London: Methuen & Co.)
1907	JOB *Introduction to the Book of Job* (London: S. Wellwood)
1905–1907	ILN *The Collected Works of G. K. Chesterton: Volume XXVII:* The Illustrated London News: *1905–1907* (edited by Lawrence J. Clipper; San Francisco: Ignatius Press, 1986)
1908	ATC *All Things Considered* (London: Methuen & Co.)
1908	O *Orthodoxy* (New York: John Lane Co.)
1909	GBS *George Bernard Shaw* (New York: John Lane Co.)
1909	TRE *Tremendous Trifles* (London: Methuen & Co.)
1910	WWW *What's Wrong With the World* (London: Cassell)
1908–1910	ILN *The Collected Works of G. K. Chesterton: Volume XXVIII:* The Illustrated London News: *1908–1910* (edited by Lawrence J. Clipper; general editors: George J. Marlin, Richard P. Rabatin, and John L. Swan; San Francisco: Ignatius Press, 1987)
1911	AD *Alarms And Discursions* (London: Methuen & Co.)
1912	MM *A Miscellany of Men* (London: Methuen & Co.)
1911–1913	ILN *The Collected Works of G. K. Chesterton: Volume XXIX:* The Illustrated London News: *1911-1913* (edited

by Lawrence J. Clipper; general editors: George J. Marlin, Richard P. Rabatin, and John L. Swan; San Francisco: Ignatius Press, 1988)

1914–1916 ILN *The Collected Works of G. K. Chesterton: Volume XXX:* The Illustrated London News: *1914-1916* (edited by Lawrence J. Clipper; general editors: George J. Marlin, Richard P. Rabatin, and John L. Swan; San Francisco: Ignatius Press, 1988)

1917   UTO *Utopia of Usurers, and Other Essays* (New York: Boni & Liveright)

1920   NJ *The New Jerusalem* (London: Hodder & Stoughton)

1920   SD *The Superstition of Divorce* (New York: John Lane Co.)

1922   EUG *Eugenics and Other Evils* (New York: Dodd, Mead & Co.)

1922   ROC *The Return of Christendom* (London: G. Allen & Unwin) [Epilogue section only]

1923   FVF *Fancies Versus Fads* (London: Methuen)

1924   SF *St. Francis of Assisi* (London: Hodder & Stoughton)

1925   EM *The Everlasting Man* (New York: Dodd, Mead & Co.)

1923–1925 ILN *The Collected Works of G. K. Chesterton: Volume XXXIII:* The Illustrated London News: *1923-1925* (edited by Lawrence J. Clipper; general editors: George J. Marlin, Richard P. Rabatin, and John L. Swan; San Francisco: Ignatius Press, 1990)

1926   CCC *The Catholic Church and Conversion* (London: Burns, Oates & Washbourne)

1926   OS *The Outline of Sanity* (London: Methuen & Co.)

1926   WC *William Cobbett* (New York: Dodd, Mead and Co.)

1926–1928 ILN *The Collected Works of G. K. Chesterton: Volume XXXIV:* The Illustrated London News: *1926-1928* (edited by Lawrence J. Clipper; general editors: George J. Marlin, Richard P. Rabatin, and John L. Swan; San Francisco: Ignatius Press, 1991)

1929   TT *The Thing: Why I am a Catholic* (New York: Sheed & Ward)

1929–1931 ILN *The Collected Works of G. K. Chesterton: Volume XXXV:* The Illustrated London News: *1929-1931* (edited by Lawrence J. Clipper; general editors: George J. Marlin, Richard P. Rabatin, and John L. Swan; San Francisco: Ignatius Press, 1991)

1933   AIS *All I Survey* (London: Methuen & Co.)

1933   HAT *On Running After One's Hat and Other Whimsies* (New York: Robert M. McBride & Co.)

1933   STA *St. Thomas Aquinas* (London: Hodder & Stoughton)

1935   WEL *The Well and The Shallows* (New York: Sheed & Ward)

1936   AS *As I Was Saying* (London: Methuen & Co.)

1936   A *Autobiography* (London: Hutchinson)

1950   CM *The Common Man* (New York: Sheed & Ward)
1964   SL *The Spice of Life and Other Essays* (London: Darwen Finlayson)
1975   AWD *The Apostle and the Wild Ducks* (London: Paul Elek)

Index of Quotations Categorized by Sources

Index of Topics